Advance Praise for *The Political Economy*

"*The Political Economy of Agribusiness* by Maria Luisa Mendonça is a brilliantly written small book about a huge issue confronting humanity: agribusiness — and how it causes social problems such as land grabbing, inequality and exploitation, and provokes resistance. It is a must-read for academics and activists alike."

— Saturnino M. Borras Jr., International Institute of
Social Studies (ISS), Netherlands

"The concept of "agronegócio" is not just a translation of "agribusiness" to Portuguese. It has been a political construction, based on a narrative of modern technology, appropriation of public resources and concentration of land and wealth. Mendonça's book critically explores this historical construction in dialogue with political economy and critical agrarian studies. A piece worth reading to better understand inequality, injustice, power relations and monopoly of wealth, as well as social resistance and land struggles in contemporary Brazil."

— Sergio Sauer, professor of environment and rural development
at the University of Brasilia (FUP/UnB) and faculty member of
the Centre for Sustainable Development (CDS) and master's in
Sustainability with Traditional Peoples and Lands

The Political Economy of Agribusiness

The Political Economy of Agribusiness

A CRITICAL DEVELOPMENT PERSPECTIVE

MARIA LUISA MENDONÇA

CRITICAL DEVELOPMENT STUDIES

*This book is dedicated to social movements that are protecting
and building ecological food systems around the world*

Editing: Erin Seatter
Cover Design: John van der Woude, JVDW Designs
Printed and bound in Canada

Published in North America by Fernwood Publishing
2970 Oxford Street, Halifax, Nova Scotia, B3L 2W4
and 748 Broadway Avenue, Winnipeg, Manitoba, R3G 0X3
www.fernwoodpublishing.ca

Published in the rest of the world by Practical Action Publishing
27a Albert Street, Rugby, Warwickshire CV21 2SG, UK

Fernwood Publishing Company Limited gratefully acknowledges the financial support of the
Government of Canada through the Canada Book Fund and the Canada Council for the Arts.
We acknowledge the Province of Manitoba for support through the Manitoba Publishers
Marketing Assistance Program and the Book Publishing Tax Credit. We acknowledge the
Nova Scotia Department of Communities, Culture and Heritage for support through the
Publishers Assistance Fund.

Library and Archives Canada Cataloguing in Publication
Title: The political economy of agribusiness: a critical development perspective / Maria
Luisa Mendonça.
Names: Mendonça, Maria Luisa, 1962- author.
Series: Critical development studies; 9.
Description: Series statement: Critical development studies; 9 | Includes bibliographical
references and index.
Identifiers: Canadiana (print) 20230000363 | Canadiana (ebook) 20230000371 | ISBN
9781773635583 (softcover) | ISBN 9781773636306 (PDF)
| ISBN 9781773636290 (EPUB)
Subjects: LCSH: Agriculture—Economic aspects. | LCSH: Agricultural industries. | LCSH:
Food sovereignty.
Classification: LCC HD1415 .M46 2023 | DDC 338.1—dc23

Contents

Critical Development Studies Series

Three decades of uneven capitalist development and neoliberal globalization have devastated the economies, societies, livelihoods and lives of people around the world, especially those in societies of the Global South. Now more than ever, there is a need for a more critical, proactive approach to the study of global and development studies. The challenge of advancing and disseminating such an approach — to provide global and development studies with a critical edge — is on the agenda of scholars and activists from across Canada and the world and those who share the concern and interest in effecting progressive change for a better world.

This series provides a forum for the publication of small books in the interdisciplinary field of critical development studies — to generate knowledge and ideas about transformative change and alternative development. The editors of the series welcome the submission of original manuscripts that focus on issues of concern to the growing worldwide community of activist scholars in this field. Critical development studies (CDS) encompasses a broad array of issues ranging from the sustainability of the environment and livelihoods, the political economy and sociology of social inequality, alternative models of local and community-based development, the land and resource-grabbing dynamics of extractive capital, the subnational and global dynamics of political and economic power, and the forces of social change and resistance, as well as the contours of contemporary struggles against the destructive operations and ravages of capitalism and imperialism in the twenty-first century.

The books in the series are designed to be accessible to an activist readership as well as the academic community. The intent is to publish a series of small books (54,000 words, including bibliography, endnotes, index and front matter) on some of the biggest issues in the interdisciplinary field of critical development studies. To this end, activist scholars from across the world in the field of development studies and related academic disciplines are invited to submit a proposal or the draft of a book that conforms to the stated aim of the series. The editors will consider the submission of complete manuscripts within the 54,000-word limit. Potential authors are encouraged to submit a proposal that includes a rationale and short synopsis of the book, an outline of proposed chapters, one or two sample chapters, and a brief biography of the author(s).

Series Editors

HENRY VELTMEYER is a research professor at Universidad Autónoma de Zacatecas (Mexico) and professor emeritus of International Development Studies at Saint Mary's University (Canada), with a specialized interest in Latin American development. He is also co-chair of the Critical Development Studies Network and a co-editor of Fernwood's Agrarian Change and Peasant Studies series. The CDS *Handbook: Tools for Change* (Fernwood, 2011) was published in French by University of Ottawa Press as *Des outils pour le changement : Une approche critique en études du développement* and in Spanish as *Herramientas para el Cambio*, with funding from Oxfam UK by CIDES, Universidad Mayor de San Andrés, La Paz, Bolivia.

ANNETTE AURÉLIE DESMARAIS is the Canada Research Chair in Human Rights, Social Justice and Food Sovereignty at the University of Manitoba (Canada). She is the author of *La Vía Campesina: Globalization and the Power of Peasants* (Fernwood, 2007), which has been republished in French, Spanish, Korean, Italian and Portuguese, and *Frontline Farmers: How the National Farmers Union Resists Agribusiness and Creates our New Food Future* (Fernwood, 2019). She is co-editor of *Food Sovereignty: Reconnecting Food, Nature and Community* (Fernwood, 2010); *Food Sovereignty in Canada: Creating Just and Sustainable Food Systems* (Fernwood, 2011); and *Public Policies for Food Sovereignty: Social Movements and the State* (Routledge, 2017).

RAÚL DELGADO WISE is a research professor and director of the PhD program in Development Studies at the Universidad Autónoma de Zacatecas (Mexico). He holds the prestigious UNESCO Chair on Migration and Development and is executive director of the International Migration and Development Network, as well as author and editor of some twenty books and more than a hundred essays. He is a member of the Mexican Academy of Sciences and editor of the book series, Latin America and the New World Order, for Miguel Angel Porrúa publishers and chief editor of the journal *Migración y Desarrollo*. He is also a member of the international working group, People's Global Action on Migration Development and Human Rights.

Acknowledgments

The Political Economy of Agribusiness: A Critical Development Perspective combines my grassroots work and my academic research on national and global policies that shape economic, social, environmental and territorial dynamics in the countryside. The book is dedicated to the amazing activists and educators from social movements and rural communities who have been an inspiration to me, especially La Vía Campesina, Movimento Sem Terra (MST, the Landless Workers' Movement), Comissão Pastoral da Terra (Pastoral Land Commission), Movimento dos Atingidos por Barragens (Movement of People Affected by Dams), Movimento de Mulheres Camponesas (Movement of Peasant Women), Movimento de Pequenos Agricultores (Movement of Small Farmers), as well as Indigenous and Quilombola (rural Afro-Brazilian) communities that are at the centre of geopolitical struggles to defend land and natural resources.

When I was planning the scope of this project, the recommendation I received from rural movements was to produce theoretical information that would uncover key contradictions about agribusiness that could be used as tools for building perspectives for change. This was the main goal of my research for my PhD in Human Geography at the University of São Paulo, which is an interdisciplinary department that combines political economy, philosophy and social sciences. I was fortunate to have Ariovaldo Umbelino de Oliveira as my adviser. One of the most influential geographers in Brazil, Ariovaldo has shaped current critical theory and mentored a whole generation of scholars in different regions of the country. He challenged me to always go back to classic political economy and philosophical questions as a way to push the theoretical envelope. I received enormous support from other professors in the Geography Department, especially from my dear friends Larissa Mies Bombardi and Marta Inez Medeiros Marques. Another space that contributed to the formulations in the book was the reading group organized by Dr. Anselmo Alfredo, who kept alive a tradition of collective theoretical debates started by Florestan Fernandes at the University of São Paulo.

My collaboration with colleagues, especially Fábio Pitta, Daniela Stefano and Carlos Vinicius Xavier, was fundamental for advancing this research. While investigating the expansion of sugarcane plantations for the production of ethanol in Brazil, we identified a new trend of financial speculation on farmland involving international pension funds. I also would like to express my deep gratitude to friends at the Comissão Pastoral da Terra who have been part of this work for many years: Marluce Melo, Tiago Thorlby, Plácido Junior and Altamiran Ribeiro. The core support for our research comes from my long-term colleagues at Rede Social de Justiça e Direitos Humanos (Network for Social Justice and Human Rights): Sandra Fae, Aton Fon Filho, Roberto Rainha, Claudia Felippe and Juliana Soares.

Since we always combine our research with national and international activism, we have been building a coalition of organizations in Brazil, the United States, Canada and Europe to stop land-grabbing by financial corporations and to support affected communities in rural areas. Our coalition has been a key space for doing public education and advocacy about critical issues related to land and food systems. I would like to thank the international organizations and activists who have been building this group, especially Lydia Simas, Jovanna García Soto, Chung-Wha Hong, Devlin Kuyek, Tristan Quinn-Thibodeau, Doug Hertzler, Jordan Treakle, Lisa Griffith, Jeff Conant, Saulo Araujo, Hannah Weinronk and Andrew Kang Bartlett.

We launched our first collective publication in 2015 together with the Center for Place, Culture and Politics at the CUNY Graduate Center, when Director Ruth W. Gilmore brought together activists and scholars to discuss similar patterns of land speculation in rural and urban areas. Since that time, Ruthie has been an inspiration, a mentor and a sister to me. The Center for Place, Culture and Politics has been a second home for me in New York, and I am grateful for the wonderful support of Mary Taylor, Peter Hitchcock and David Harvey. At seminars I met brilliant people who formed a community of friends, including Sonia Borges, Mamyrah Prosper, Ujju Aggarwal, Kafui Attoh, Laura Y. Liu and Leigh Claire La Berge.

Over the years, I have had the privilege of working with amazing scholars and activists from different countries. Special thanks to Peter Rosset, Shalmali Guttal, Mary Ann Manahan, Sofia Monsalve, Walden Bello, Raj Patel and Hector Mondragon for our collaboration on the Land Research Action Network and the Global Campaign for Agrarian Reform that, together with La Vía Campesina, produced timely information about international land and food policies in support of grassroots movements in Africa, Asia and Latin America.

I am grateful for all the conversations and references that contributed to this book. A very special note of appreciation to Mônica Dias Martins, Cecilia MacDowell Santos, Guilherme Delgado, Mônica Leite Lessa, Kit Miller, João Pedro Stédile, Brian Garvey, Jaime Alves, Cliff Welch, Biorn Maybury-Lewis, Ricardo Rezende Figueira, Nikhil Aziz and Gerardo Cerdas. I would like to thank Wendy Wolford and Philip McMichael for receiving me as a visiting scholar at Cornell University, where I did the historical research for the book. During that time, I was practically living at the Cornell library, as the first person to arrive in the morning and the last one to leave at night. I also would like to express my gratitude to Karen Lang for her invaluable feedback on the final manuscript.

At Fernwood Publishing, I would like to thank the commitment and attention of the editors and the staff, especially Errol Sharpe, Jessica Herdman, Beverley Rach, and Erin Seatter.

I know these acknowledgments are incomplete because this book is a result of a collective journey that involved many wonderful people. I am very grateful for the care and support of my family, my son Luiz and my *companheiro* Marcelo, who kept me grounded with their love during this process.

Acronyms

BNDES	National Bank for Economic and Social Development
CEDAW	United Nations Committee on the Elimination of Discrimination Against Women
CPCP	Center for Place, Culture and Politics
CPT	Pastoral Land Commission
ECLAC	United Nations Economic Commission for Latin America and the Caribbean
FAO	Food and Agriculture Organization of the United Nations
GATT	General Agreement on Tariffs and Trade
GDP	gross domestic product
HMC	Harvard University Management Company
INCRA	National Institute for Agrarian Reform
LAAD	Latin American Agribusiness Development Corporation
MST	Landless Workers Movement
TIAA	Teachers Insurance and Annuity Association
TRS	total recoverable sugar
USAID	US Agency for International Development
USDA	US Department of Agriculture
WTO	World Trade Organization

Introduction

This book is the result of several years of grassroots work with rural movements in Brazil, and a contribution to their strategy of exposing the main dynamics that frame economic and geopolitical disputes in the countryside. In order to understand this process, it is necessary to start with a historical analysis of the creation of agribusiness as a concept and as a set of policies in the United States, as well as its international influence. The book explores theoretical perspectives that explain the political economy of agribusiness from a critical development approach. It describes recent international policies that play a key role in agricultural systems in Brazil, such as financial speculation in farmland, agroenergy production and market concentration of commodities.

The historical analysis investigates how the image of agribusiness was shaped by the publication of the 1957 book *A Concept of Agribusiness* by John Davis and Ray Goldberg at Harvard University. This book had a strong influence on agricultural policies in the United States and internationally. It promoted a "technological revolution" supported by the state to provide incentives for large farms and massive processing, distribution and transportation infrastructure for the production of food and fibres. The agribusiness system envisioned by Davis and Goldberg included agricultural and industrial corporations, research institutions, lobby groups and state offices.

During the post–World War II period in the United States, the economic context was characterized by a crisis of overaccumulation. In the agriculture sector, this included an increase in the productivity of grains, which demanded larger investments to cover the costs of mechanization, and the creation of several governmental policies to provide subsidies for internal markets and for export. These policies, described in the first chapter, reveal how the state has played a central role in the creation and expansion of the agribusiness system.

The internationalization of the agribusiness system by the United States resulted in the expansion of monocrop plantations of agricultural commodities in several countries. The case of Brazil, presented in the book, illustrates this dynamic. To expand the influence of agribusiness, the United States flooded international markets with its surplus of grains and supported the growing role of US agribusiness corporations internationally through trade policies and financial mechanisms. As a result of this type of neocolonial approach, US agribusiness corporations took control of world grain stocks and commercialization, which stimulated financial speculation in agricultural commodities.

The discourse in defence of the development of agribusiness was promoted within an ideological context influenced by the so-called evolutionary economy, which is based on the idea that economic theory and technological "progress" should follow patterns similar to biological science. However, the crisis of overaccumulation revealed contradictions in the process of industrializing agriculture, which increased constant capital in relation to labour exploitation in the production process. The second chapter of the book presents an economic analysis of this process, as well as the main theoretical concepts that are helpful for understanding the historical and current dynamics of power relations in rural areas. One perspective in this analysis is the theory of value, which is based on the main categories of capitalist social relations: labour, capital and land.

In general terms, capital is defined as the result of extracting value from labour in the production process as well as in distribution, circulation of commodities and financial markets. Capitalism is an economic system mostly mediated by the commodity form, which is based on exchange value or market dynamics, as opposed to use value, which is not measured by markets. The global expansion of capitalism promotes the commodification of all aspects of life. For example, water is an essential element of life, which means that it has high use value, but its commodification has influenced monopolist control of this market to generate exchange value. In the current dynamics of capitalist relations, use value and exchange value form a dialectical unit. This theoretical approach permeates the book, as it investigates how agribusiness corporations promote the commodification of land and other natural resources.

The analysis of agribusiness demonstrates how the process of capital reproduction in search of valorization or profits leads to capital accumulation. The book describes these dynamics of capital reproduction as agribusiness corporations tend to increase the concentration of constant capital or fixed assets (such as land, machinery, technology and raw materials). It also shows how this trend relates to labour exploitation as the source of surplus value or profit. The search for profit or valorization is the main driving force of capitalist accumulation and the development of productive forces.

In *The Wealth of Nations*, Adam Smith identified labour as a source of value and as a measure of exchange value based on the naturalization of the division of labour. He explained the division of labour as a natural inclination for exchange in social relations, which would lead to the development of productive forces, combining less labour time with a higher volume of commodities produced through labour specialization and production mechanization. For Smith, the "law of supply and demand" would follow a "natural order" moved by individual interests that would eventually benefit society.

David Ricardo developed the theory of value in the book *On the Principles of Political Economy and Taxation*. He analyzed value as exchange value, measured by the comparative number of commodities produced by labour in relation to fixed capital. The relative value of commodities is therefore determined by labour time. Ricardo saw the increase in productivity of the means of subsistence (such as food, shoes and clothes) as key to determining the reproduction of the labour force. According to his theory, value originates in the productive process, in addition to the commercialization of commodities. Thus, the development of productive forces would determine a difference in value, and not in the price of commodities, as social labour time defines the average profit rate. This observation is based on the proportion between fixed and circulating capital. Ricardo also related the decline in profit rate to the increase in fixed capital.

Marx defined value based on the concept of labour as a concrete abstraction and the dialectical relation between use value and exchange value. When social relations are mediated by the commodity form, use value and exchange value are merged into a dialectical unity, as opposite but inseparable concepts. For Marx, value is determined by the proportional relation between constant capital (meaning objectified or "dead" labour) and variable capital ("live" labour), considering the unity formed by the production and circulation of commodities. Marx described the capitalist division of labour by explaining the history of primitive accumulation, with reference to the violent displacement of peasants and the role of colonization. The relation between labour and means of production in peasant agriculture brings fundamental differences that are central to the current debate about the political economy of agribusiness.

These concepts are relevant to the study of agribusiness and its tendency to form monopoly capital by dominating national and international markets, as the book demonstrates. Increasing investment in constant capital is a result of competition between corporations, but it generates a contradictory dynamic of capital concentration because it reduces competition. This process includes mergers and joint ventures that eliminate smaller companies, leading to a market monopoly in agricultural production and trade. Further, agribusiness corporations increase their assets to have privileged access to credit and subsidies. Competition functions as a dialectical element in stimulating the development of productive forces through higher levels of investment in constant capital that only certain corporations with greater access to subsidies can achieve, which ends up eliminating competition.

Capital mobility creates this pattern of market concentration internationally, although with certain characteristics in different regions and countries, according to the ways it affects the appropriation of land and natural resources. A monopoly over farmland follows a dialectical tendency as well, since it "immobilizes" capital and, at the same time, stimulates land speculation and capital circulation in financial markets. The current process of speculation in farmland, described in Chapter 3, illustrates this dynamic.

The book also explains how the market concentration by agribusiness corporations reveals a contradiction within the organic composition of capital, which is formed by the dialectical relation between constant or fixed capital and variable capital or labour power. This analysis shows that a market monopoly does not arise from a linear or mechanical process, as if the development of productive forces were only a result of technological "progress." On the contrary, it demonstrates a dialectical relation between crisis and accumulation, as simultaneous and permanent elements of capitalism, even when they are manifested as polarized and cyclical.

A crisis of overaccumulation, therefore, is not just a result of underconsumption or an imbalance between supply and demand. It happens within a process where there is a proportional increase of constant capital in relation to variable capital. The search for valorization increases the composition of capital and labour productivity, which means a decrease in valorization through labour exploitation. Based on this perspective, the "product" of capitalist agriculture is expressed in the search for valorization within social relations of land, capital and labour.

To explain this process, the book describes how the agribusiness system was promoted through a set of measures implemented by governments and private institutions that intensified the industrialization and standardization of agriculture in several countries. Some of the key elements of this system are the uniformity of crops, the application of machinery and chemical inputs and the heavy use of water and energy in the production process.

The agribusiness system also relies on subsidies and state credit to cover increasing costs of production with mechanization. The internationalization of agribusiness led to capital concentration in industrial supplies and trade corporations.

The origins of this system of production date back to the Great Depression of the 1930s, when the US government adopted measures to restrict food imports and protect local agriculture. These policies included subsidies for both food production and price guarantees, which generated surpluses, especially of grains. As a result, the government began to provide funding for export and for "food aid" programs that promoted dumping in other countries and flooded the world grain market. In the 1970s, US-based agribusiness corporations intensified their efforts to establish subsidiary companies in various countries. Financial deregulation facilitated this process by increasing the international mobility of capital. The growing specialization of agricultural production led farmworkers and peasants to migrate, which changed land ownership structures and land uses in many countries.

Widespread use of machinery and chemical inputs caused genetic erosion of crops, deterioration of soils and speculation on land prices. Data on the loss of soil fertility are generally omitted from official statistics. However, growing dependency on nitrogen-based fertilizers reveals how natural nutrients are being depleted. The use of inputs based on fossil fuels causes major impacts on water sources and air quality. It also generates economic vulnerability in a context marked by geopolitical disputes over oil and natural gas, as well as instability caused by the role these commodities play in speculative operations on financial markets.

The historical and current policies discussed in the book are key elements to understanding the causes of the global environmental crisis and climate change. The book also highlights the organizing process of rural communities in Brazil to build international solidarity in defence of land rights and ecological food production. Brazilian rural movements have a long history of struggle against land-grabbing and the expansion of monocrop plantations by agribusiness.

Before the word "agribusiness" became popular in Brazil, the most frequently used concept was "agroindustrial complex," associated with linear notions of "progress," "development" and technological "advancement." After the 1960s, Brazilian agriculture became more dependent on industrial inputs and continued to prioritize foreign markets. To cover the increasing costs of machinery and chemical inputs, controlled by multinational corporations, more access to credit and subsidies for agricultural production was required. The so-called agroindustrial complex was supported by state policies such as special lines of credit that deepened the role of financial capital in agriculture.

To explain the process of transformation in Brazilian agriculture, the book includes original research about key words that constructed the concept of agribusiness in mainstream media outlets. This research shows a change in mainstream discourse, especially in relation to the dissemination of key words to describe the predominant agricultural system, based on social, economic and political elements used to promote the concept of agribusiness. Particularly during the implementation of neoliberal policies in the 1990s, academic institutions and media outlets associated the concepts of agribusiness and "production chains" so that industrial, chemical and marketing businesses would be included in the calculation of agriculture's contribution to gross domestic product (GDP). At that time, agribusiness corporations also advanced the idea that family farmers should be "integrated" into these "chains."

Meanwhile, neoliberal policies facilitated the international circulation of financial capital, as well as speculation in commodities markets. Structural adjustment policies in Brazil stimulated the dumping of agricultural products from external markets and the privatization of strategic economic sectors. Neoliberal policies were based on the defence of a "minimum state," even though large agriculture corporations have always depended on several forms of governmental subsidy. This is a main point of investigation explored in the book, which examines the creation of the agribusiness system in the United States and its international expansion.

Agribusiness corporations in Brazil lobby for increasing access to state subsidies while also complaining about "protectionist" policies and agricultural subsidies in other countries, especially in the United States and Europe. The agribusiness lobby in Brazil occupies key spaces of power in the national congress. A common element in its discourse is the idea that Brazil has a "vocation" for agricultural production, associated with the notion of "development" as a linear historical process based on technological "progress." This discourse is used to justify the demand for state subsidies for large monocrop plantations as part of the "production chains" of agribusiness. The book highlights this dynamic as it describes how the agribusiness system was promoted in Brazil, including through state policies to expand sugarcane plantations for the production of ethanol.

The word "development" is frequently used by Brazilian government officials, corporations and media outlets to describe the expansion of agribusiness (Mendonça 2018). This is part of a strategy to disseminate a positive image and to hide the impacts of an agricultural system based on monocrop plantations that destroy natural resources, such as land and water. A key objective of this strategy for agribusiness corporations is to have continuing access to state subsidies. These subsidies become a means for private corporations to appropriate public funds. Their main "product," then, is debt. This is one of the primary points investigated in the book, along with how agribusiness corporations take advantage of subsidized credit to speculate in farmland and in financial markets.

To justify receiving state subsidies and special credit, the agribusiness sector claims it contributes to economic "development." This type of discourse is an essential part of a communications strategy used to increase agribusiness corporations' control over land, perpetuating social and economic inequalities in rural areas. Historically, the agricultural system based on extensive monocropping of commodities for export has relied on state policies that generate public debt. In 1980, for example, the Brazilian government "forgave" a US$13-billion debt of agribusiness corporations. This represented twice the amount of the trade balance for agriculture at that time. Indebtedness persisted for agribusinesses, despite their continued access to various types of subsidies and tax incentives. In 1999, the Brazilian government cancelled another US$18 billion in debt, when the announced trade surplus for the agribusiness sector was US$10 billion (Mendonça 2018).

Even during periods of economic crisis, the Brazilian government has continued to provide large subsidies for agribusiness. In 2015, for example, subsidized credit provided by the state program called Plano Safra increased 20 percent compared to the previous year and reached a total of R$180 billion (R$, or the real, is the Brazilian currency). Data from the Ministry of Agriculture show that this amount was equivalent to the trade balance of agribusiness in 2014, which was US$80 billion (at an average exchange rate of R$2.50 to each US$). This number does not include agribusiness debts, which have been accumulating for years. In the 2014–15 harvest period, the debt of sugar and ethanol corporations alone exceeded R$50 billion, which represented a 12 percent increase compared to the previous year's debt (Mendonça 2015).

In addition to increasing debt and dependency on subsidized credit to cover the rising costs of machinery and chemical inputs, state support for agribusiness deepened Brazil's role as a supplier of agricultural raw materials based on foreign demand. Meanwhile, the import of industrialized food products changed eating habits in the country. Today, there is a growing demand for organic and locally produced food in Europe and in the United

States. In Brazil, food production by small farmers is usually underestimated and often even ignored in economic data, despite their role of providing food for the majority of the population.

The Brazilian government spends huge amounts of public resources to finance the production of agricultural commodities, which constitute an increasingly limited list of products for export. For the harvest period of 2021–22, for example, the Brazilian government announced that its subsidized credit plan, Plano Safra, would allocate R$39.34 billion (equivalent to about US$8 billion) to small farmers from a total of R$251.22 billion, while the Brazilian Institute of Geography and Statistics estimates that small farmers produce approximately 70 percent of food for local markets in the country (Ministério da Agricultura 2021).

The combination of historical, analytical and field research presented in the book serves as a tool for grassroots organizing and international solidarity to transform agricultural systems, replacing monocrop plantations of commodities with agroecological food production. This movement includes strengthening the role of peasant and small farmers who produce healthy food for local markets and defending the land rights of Indigenous and Quilombola communities to build food sovereignty.

1 The Concept of Agribusiness

The concept of agribusiness is related to a series of measures implemented by governments and private institutions that intensified the industrialization and standardization of agriculture around the world. After World War II, the United States led the expansion of agricultural markets, which was accompanied by the acceleration of the industrialization of agriculture mainly through the mechanization of production and the growing application of chemical inputs. This system increased the costs of production and generated greater demand for state credit and subsidies. State support for agribusiness resulted in increasing market concentration, with multinational corporations controlling most of the production of industrial inputs and the international trading of agricultural commodities.

The term "agribusiness" was created at the Harvard Graduate School of Business Administration with the publication of the 1957 book *A Concept of Agribusiness*, by John Davis and Ray Goldberg. The main premise of the book was that the countryside would go through major changes due to a "technological revolution" based on scientific "progress" in agriculture. According to this view, public policies to support large-scale agriculture would be needed because of the increase in the cost of production, transportation, processing and distribution of food and fibres.

The authors' influence was not restricted to the academic world. It went so far as to affect government policy in the United States and in other countries.[1] Davis was the assistant secretary of agriculture during the Eisenhower administration and president of the Commodity Credit Corporation. He also organized a series of delegations to intervene in international conferences. His goal as a Harvard professor was to "[launch] a major effort to reshape American thinking about the nation's agriculture" (Davis and Hinshaw 1957: 10).

Davis and Goldberg argued that agriculture has been conceived as an integral part of industrial production for more than 150 years, as peasants used to produce not only their own food but also their equipment, supplies, fuel, housing, clothing and household utensils. The main change on "modern farms" was that they stopped being self-sufficient and began to function as a business based on monocropping of agricultural commodities. Activities such as processing, storage and distribution were transferred to other corporations, many of which produced industrial products such as tractors, trucks, fuel, fertilizers, feed and pesticides. According to the authors, the proposal to use the term "agribusiness" emerged because "our vocabulary did not keep up with the pace of progress." This "progress," as they described it, meant that "our farms would not be able to function for even a week if these services were cut off" (Davis and Goldberg 1957: 2).

The "drive for mechanized agriculture" created growing dependency on industrial inputs such as machines, tractors and the chemical fertilizers used to compensate for the loss of soil fertility. This process demanded large amounts of energy and stimulated the expansion of oil production. At the same time, the genetic engineering industry started to develop genetically modified seeds and artificial insemination methods. This contributed, on the one hand, to the segmentation of agricultural production and, on the other, to the construction of large industrial monopolies that appropriated income from land. Included in Davis and Goldberg's conceptualization of the "agribusiness" system are landowners, business associations, research institutions, universities, lobby groups and the government, which had the function of supporting research and establishing regulatory and trade policies.

According to Davis and Goldberg (1957: 8), agribusiness accounted for 35 to 50 percent of the US economy in the early 1950s. To arrive at these numbers, they calculated the total amount that US consumers spent in 1954 on food, beverages, tobacco, shoes, clothing and accessories. Spending on all these items added up to close to US$93 billion, or 40 percent of total consumption for that year (US$236.5 billion). The breakdown of these calculations is as follows: processed food, $26.3 billion; unprocessed food, $10 billion; spending in restaurants, $16.4 billion; textiles, $11 billion; leather products, $3 billion; alcoholic beverages, $1.5 billion; wool and paper, $3 billion; tobacco, $2.8 billion; wholesale and exports, $15 billion; and other items, $3 billion.

Similar percentages can be found in the case of Brazil. The weight of Brazilian agribusiness in the economy is estimated at 35 to 40 percent when the chains of production — both on- and off-farm production — are included. The concept of agribusiness includes everything from the production of chemical and industrial inputs to commercialization and wholesale companies. This formula leads researchers to overestimate agriculture's role in the GDP and does not take into consideration the various types of public subsidies granted to the sector, nor the economic, social and environmental liabilities that agribusiness generates (Mendonça 2018).

Davis and Goldberg mentioned "negative factors" and expressed concern with "mismatches and imbalances" in "evolutionary progress" that introduced "complex problems" between "commercial farms and poor peasant families." When analyzing changes in the economic structure of US agriculture from 1947 to 1954, they found that the number of workers employed in agriculture remained stable at close to twenty-four million but declined from 41 percent to 37 percent as a portion of the total labour force. Furthermore, there was a considerable increase in the costs of production: 111 percent for machinery, 70 percent for operating vehicles, 57 percent for fertilizers, 35 percent for seeds and 59 percent for labour. Sales in the sector grew 56 percent in absolute terms, but the profit margin decreased 19 percent. The study cites data on the "Realized Return per Hour to All Farm Labour and Management" — that is, the rate of social surplus value in the sector, which dropped 25.5 percent between 1947 and 1954 (Davis and Goldberg 1957: 6–15).

These data illustrate a propensity for crises of overproduction to occur in industrial agriculture, characterized by an increase in the costs of inputs in relation to the labour time needed for production. This is not due to an increase in supply and a decrease in demand, but rather to the disproportionate amount of fixed capital used for production in relation to the labour force employed in agriculture.

The Industrialization of Agriculture in the United States and the Expansion of World Trade

In the nineteenth century, mechanical technologies were introduced into agriculture to increase labour productivity. The mechanization of agriculture began in the 1900s with the use of large tractors and became more widespread with the production of smaller tractors powered by automobile engines, which Henry Ford began to develop in 1908. The monopoly over the manufacturing of farm machinery established over a century ago exists today. Four companies (Deere, International Harvester, Massey Ferguson and the Ford Motor Company) control 99 percent of the global market.

The principal changes in the twentieth century were mostly related to biological and chemical technologies, whose use intensified after World

War II. Between 1940 and 1946, the price of agricultural products on the international market jumped 138 percent. This level was maintained in the postwar period due to interventions of the US government that established price guarantees for farmers in the domestic market and generated additional external demand through "food aid" policies (Cochrane 1993: 124).

Between 1933 and 1970, US farmers replaced more than 50 percent of inputs produced on their farms with industrialized products, which generated a 212 percent increase in the use of machines and 1,800 percent jump in the use of chemical inputs. During the same period, the number of farmworkers declined by over 70 percent. The productivity of the main commercial plantations did not grow at the same rate. Data from the US Department of Agriculture (USDA) show that from 1870 to 1940, agricultural production remained at similar levels. The yield per acre for wheat went from 12.7 tons in 1870 to 15.7 tons in 1950, corn went from 26.1 tons in 1870 to 37.8 tons in 1950 and cotton increased from 174.2 tons in 1870 to 273.4 tons in 1950. While productivity continued to increase after 1950, it appears to have stabilized in 1970, when yield per acre was 31.8 tons for wheat, 80.8 tons for corn and 436.7 tons for cotton. Between 1950 and 1981, international trade in agriculture expanded 14 percent. US agricultural exports rose 22 percent, from US$6.7 billion in 1970 to US$44 billion in 1981. The volume of US exports went from 60 million tons to 160 million tons during this period. The country became the largest exporter of grain — namely, wheat, corn and soybean — on the world market. This increase in exports was primarily due to agribusiness corporations' easy access to credit, the availability of so-called petrodollars and the growth in the Soviet Union's demand for grain (Cochrane 1993: 128–32).

USDA data from 1976 reveal that Japan was the largest importer of agricultural products from the United States, importing US$3.3 billion worth of goods annually. The Soviet Union came in second, with imports amounting to US$1.86 billion a year. Other major importers were the Netherlands (US$1.76 billion), East Germany (US$1.62 billion) and Canada (US$1.4 billion). Brazil came in thirteenth place in the list of countries importing grains from the United States and was its main market in Latin America, with the equivalent of US$430 million in annual agricultural imports (Rawlins 1980: 12).

Even during the "oil crisis" in the 1970s, guaranteeing the availability of fuel for agribusiness in the United States was a priority. In 1977, the US agricultural industry spent US$85 billion on petrochemicals. The amount spent on workers' salaries was US$54 billion and packaging costs were US$15 billion (Rawlins 1980: 22–25). Industrial supplies used in agricultural production have a strategic influence on US exports. Some of the main commodities linked to the international trade of agribusiness are oil and fertilizers. Other related companies include the ones in the processing, wholesale, transportation and shipping sectors. In 1990, US agricultural exports added up to US$39.3 billion, whereas the cost of industrial supplies used in agriculture was estimated at US$62.8 billion (Rosson 1994: 13).

The growing industrialization of agriculture demanded an increase in credit to cover the costs of industrial inputs. This process was stimulated in the United States by the creation of the Farm Credit System, which provided special lines of credit and state subsidies for agricultural production and exports (Rawlins 1980: 61). Access to credit for agribusiness tripled between 1940 and 1962. During the same period, the use of chemical fertilizers doubled, as did the practice of aerial spraying. There was an increase in the standardization of crops and the concentration of land ownership, but only in relative terms, as family-owned units continued to represent the majority of the farms (Hampe, Witteberg and Edds 1980: 61–66).

In the 1990s, over a third of the country's grain production was destined for exports. In 1992, US grain exports to other countries reached a volume of US$42 billion. Sales of industrialized agribusiness products to foreign markets, which have a higher value added, also carried considerable weight in the balance of trade. The volume of these exports went from US$28 billion in the 1960s to US$240 billion in the 1990s. At the same time, the increase in US exports of processed food generated greater demand for imports of agricultural raw materials, which went from US$5.6 billion in 1970 to US$22.6 billion in 1990. These kinds of imports are considered noncompetitive, as they serve to complement materials that are not produced in the country (Rosson 1994: 6–7).

The expansion of agricultural exports in the United States was the result of protectionist measures that strengthened the domestic market and guaranteed prices for farmers, as well as environmental policies to conserve soil fertility and water resources. Since the 1930s, the US government has established measures to guarantee control over the price and volume of its agricultural production by providing farmers economic incentives to reduce production levels (through laws such as the Soil Conservation and Domestic Allotment Act of 1936), conserve the soil and turn certain areas into forest reserves. Other measures included government purchases of perishable products, the practice of dumping surplus on foreign markets and programs to stimulate the domestic food market.

The International Standardization of Food

In addition to the grain market, which plays a central role in agricultural commodities, the standardization of industrialized food was fundamental to the expansion of the agribusiness model at the international level. The US processed food industry experienced a boom during World War II, when processed food became known as "combat food" because it was used to feed soldiers abroad. The US Department of Defense created a special division called the Natick Laboratory with the goal of supporting research in this sector. Canned food was the first product the laboratory created. Later, frozen, dehydrated and precooked food and water-soluble, powdered beverages were also produced (Goldberg, Bird and Arthur 1968: 26).

The state was also the primary promoter of the creation of farm equipment, fertilizers, insecticides, transportation methods and storage for the mass distribution of these products. The main agencies involved in these activities were the Departments of Agriculture, Defense and the Interior. The priority of the Department of Agriculture was to develop research on the industrialization of food and fibres. The focus of the Department of Defense was on developing methods to freeze and dry food, food irradiation, preservation, packaging and storage, which were initially used for military purposes. It also worked on the fabrication of artificial proteins, flavours and aromas, as well as enzymes to detect bacteria. As for the Department of the Interior, its main line of work was the manipulation of fish and seafood (Goldberg, Bird and Arthur 1968: 47–49).

The US government created the National Advisory Commission on Food and Fiber to direct its agricultural policy. In *The Technological Front in the Food and Fibre Economy*, Goldberg, Bird and Arthur (1968: 2) defended the intensifying market concentration and the production of processed foods: "There will evolve new ways and means of feeding people, not only in the United States, but in developing nations as well.... New ways of processing, handling, storing, and marketing them.... There will be fewer but larger food marketing establishments. Conglomerate relationships will be much more prevalent." To expand the market of industrialized food, corporations had to invest in advertising their brands and target specific audiences. The cost of advertising in the industry increased 175 percent from US$44.6 billion in 1960 to US$124 billion in 1977 (Rawlins 1980: 158). To cover the high cost of advertising, agribusiness corporations would have to sell large volumes of their products:

> Since many of the newer processing techniques require compli-
> cated and expensive machines, the future will bring about higher

capital requirements in the food processing industry.... Both factors would tend to concentrate the industry in the hands of fewer processors. A third factor that would appear to affect competition in the future is the national promotion of brand processed foods.... A brand is a powerful tool — especially if the brand is advertised using the high-pressure techniques of national TV programs. Thus, branded items not only have to be sold nationwide; they have to be sold in large volumes to justify their high promotional costs. (Goldberg, Bird and Arthur 1968: 21)

The report also included recommendations to the US government regarding foreign policy. The authors predicted that the United States would continue to be involved in wars, which would increase global demand and the price of food. It proposed "food aid" programs as a way of dumping agricultural surpluses from the United States on other countries along with contractual guarantees for US corporations operating abroad. These food aid programs, promoted by the US government nationally and internationally, played a key role in the expansion of agribusiness: "The Federal Government has instituted many programmes to aid the less fortunate members of our society. Programmes designed for improving their diet will in turn provide a growing market for farm products.... Helping feed the people of underdeveloped countries will become important in the years ahead" (Goldberg, Bird and Arthur 1968: 3). Other recommendations included increasing requirements for food standardization and quality control restrictions, which would hinder the diversification of production and imports from other countries.

The authors defended the standardization of food and its monopolization by agribusiness corporations as a way to deal with the supposed need to reduce the workforce and the pressure from farmworkers to increase wages and benefits:

> Rising wages and additional fringe benefits of labor in developed countries, including the United States, will keep pressure on the cost structures and this factor will also accelerate the trend towards optimized firms.... The main changes to be anticipated are more labor-saving devices; relatively less labor used; and more capital investment in buildings, equipment, and facilities. Firms will be larger and more specialized. (Goldberg, Bird and Arthur 1968: 3)

The report indicated that market expansion of processed food would encourage the purchase of refrigerators, freezers, microwave ovens and other household appliances, such as can openers, grinders, blenders and electric knives. This process would involve the automation of services via fast-food restaurants, drive-ins, vending machines and more. In short, it brought structural changes to the food industry, including a higher rate of mechanization, a greater need to invest capital in equipment and infrastructure and the concentration of capital through mergers and acquisitions, even across sectors, such as food, tobacco, distribution, aluminum and electronics. A system of mass food production also required large investments in advertising to promote certain brands, which large corporations made thanks to their access to credit and subsidies. The internationalization of the food industry drove the expansion of the agribusiness system based on production "chains" that include industrial inputs and mass distribution in multinational retail corporations or supermarkets.

The purpose of the internationalization of processed food corporations was to "guarantee economies of scale, be able to access the biggest lines of credit, take advantage of managers, facilitate entry into new markets, protect through broader markets in geographic terms and compete more efficiently" (Hampe, Witteberg and Edds 1980: 8–11). The food distribution and retail sectors became increasingly monopolistic. Between 1950 and 1960, the number of supermarkets doubled, and their sales quadrupled, representing 70 percent of the US wholesale market. This process was accompanied by the standardization of food and the growing influence of advertising agencies in promoting certain brands of processed products (Hampe, Witteberg and Edds 1980: 328).

Economic and Geopolitical Contradictions in the Expansion of Agribusiness

The industrialization of agriculture in the United States and the internationalization of agribusiness generated a growing demand for governmental credit and subsidies for local production and exports. Approved in 1954, Public Law 480 allowed importing countries to acquire US grains in their local currency. This measure mainly benefited agribusiness corporations that used the new policy to establish operations in several countries. This increased food dependency among these countries, as local producers were forced to compete with large foreign corporations. This policy also served to benefit the geopolitical interests of the US government. In Asia, for example, priority was given to funding the grain purchases of South Vietnam and South Korea, as well as the Ferdinando Marcos regime in the Philippines. In the Middle East, "food aid" was fundamental in US efforts to win Egypt's support for opposition to the creation of the Palestinian state. In Latin America, this policy served to strengthen Augusto Pinochet's regime in Chile (Burbach and Flynn 1980: 70–77).

Agricultural exports became a key component of US economy and foreign policy. In the postwar period, the country controlled half of the total volume of world grain exports. In addition to European and Japanese markets, considered priorities during the postwar "reconstruction" period, access to the Soviet market was fundamental to the United States. In 1972, the Soviet Union imported eighteen million tons of wheat from the United States — one-quarter of the wheat harvested in the United States that year. This led to a major increase in the price of agricultural commodities, which favoured agribusiness, especially corporations such as Cargill, Continental Grain, Dreyfus and Cook Industries (Burbach and Flynn 1980: 50–52).

In the years that followed, the United States signed an agreement that guaranteed that it would export a minimum of six million tons of grains a year to the Soviet Union. In 1979, US corn and wheat exports to the Soviet market reached twenty-five million tons (Burbach and Flynn 1980: 60). At the end of the following year, due to the escalation of conflict in Afghanistan, the Jimmy Carter administration suspended the agreement and began to buy the surplus of farmers who depended on the Soviet market. The interruption of grain exports to the Soviet Union had major impacts during the 1980s, a period marked by a decline in US agricultural production. Another determining factor was the increasing costs of production, especially because of the intensive use of chemical fertilizers and other oil-based inputs.

In addition to playing a central role in US foreign policy, the agribusiness industry has influenced the country's migration laws since the beginning of the twentieth century. In 1917, the government adopted measures to facilitate the hiring of Mexican migrants, especially in California. In 1920, an estimated 70,000 Mexican workers were in California, and this number reached 400,000 in 1940. During World War II, an agreement between the Mexican and the US governments created the *bracero* program, which stimulated a new wave of migration of rural workers. In 1965, the number of *braceros* in the United States was as high as 450,000, and they constituted the majority of the labour force in rural areas. These workers were hired directly by the government, not by the companies, during the harvest season. They were confronted with degrading working conditions and lived in makeshift housing. The program, which began in 1942, continued on throughout the so-called golden age, which is characterized by the modernization of US agribusiness. During the program's twenty-five years, *braceros'* "wages increased from US$0.75 to only US$1.25 per hour. One of the main purposes of the program was to maintain [the pay of] rural workers" at a minimum level (Walker 2004: 71–72).

In the 1970s, another strategy of the US government was to try to advance the negotiations of the General Agreement on Tariffs and Trade with the goal of obtaining the best possible advantages for its agricultural exports. A key goal of the United States during the negotiations was to maintain control over world grain reserves. If successful, it could speculate on these commodities to stimulate increases in exports at times when prices were high on the international market and promote dumping in other countries when the scenario was one of falling prices. Despite the dissemination of neoliberal discourse at the time, state support for US agriculture reached its highest level in decades. Then the world recession in the 1980s damaged US agricultural exports — they dropped to less than $26 billion by 1986. The government's response was to adopt a new set of laws, known as the Food Security Act, with the objective of increasing subsidies. The US government also maintained an exchange rate policy that was favourable to its exports (Rosson 1994: 3–5). The world economic recession exposed agribusiness's dependency on state subsidies:

> By 1984, interest cost per acre for producing corn in the United States was fast approaching the fertilizer cost per acre and depending on the terms of trade within the agribusiness system, many commercial producers have been caught in a cost-price squeeze with a high break-even for their farming operations. Government price policies become even more critical, as the commercial producer and farm supplier, as well as the processor and distributor of subsidized export value-added products, have not only their profitability at stake but their very survival. Of all the factors noted so far, the dollar exchange rate would seem to be one of the most important factors affecting US competitiveness in a price-sensitive global agricultural commodity market. (Goldberg 1985: 17)

Mechanization and the use of petrochemical products inflate the costs of monocropping-based agricultural production. This practice decreases the natural fertility of soils and productivity levels. In response, farmers are required to spend more resources on chemical inputs, which generates higher levels of debt. Also, privileged access to state credit and subsidies contributes to market concentration in agriculture: "These huge industrial-style operations are thriving not because they are more productive (they are, in fact, far less productive), but because they are systematically supported by government policies" (Hodge, Merrifield and Gorelick 2002: 8). Prioritizing subsidies for agribusiness, at the expense of smallholder farmers, is part of state policy in the United States and in other countries. Data from 2002 show that in the United States, 10 percent of farmers receive two-thirds of subsidies. In England, 80 percent of subsidies go to 20 percent of the biggest agricultural corporations (Hodge, Merrifield and Gorelick 2002: 5–7).

Globally, market concentration stimulated agribusiness corporations to create strategies of vertical and horizontal integration such as complete mergers between companies, as well as contractual partnerships that signed trade agreements between sectors of a particular supply chain. In the 1970s, these mergers increased, for example, between production and distribution companies and between transportation and marketing companies. In the United States, land concentration did not happen in the same way. A significant number of small and medium farms continued to play an important role in the sector, even though the number of large farms was on the rise due to the growing need for capitalization to cover the costs of mechanization.

The global economic crisis at the end of the 1970s generated instability in commodity markets and stimulated mergers between corporations and the further monopolization of agribusiness. Some examples were the mergers of ADM, Intrade and Toepfer, and of Continental Grain and A.E. Staley. One of the main changes in the agribusiness structure at that time was increasing concentration of private corporations in trading markets, which until then were largely controlled by government agencies (Goldberg 1985: 12). Market concentration also increased in other sectors during the 1970s. In 1979, 60 percent of the production of chemical inputs was concentrated in fifteen companies, 68 percent of processed foods were produced by forty-nine companies and 77 percent of wholesales were controlled by forty-four companies (Vogeler 1981: 106).

The Internationalization of Agribusiness

The drive for the internationalization of agribusiness originated in Mexico in 1945, when the International Maize and Wheat Improvement Center began to monopolize research on seeds. The standardization of seeds was crucial to the success of the new "technology package," as the cultivation of native species did not require intensive chemical use. Throughout the 1960s, other institutions with the same purpose were created, such as the International Rice Research Institute in the Philippines, the International Center for Tropical Agriculture in Colombia and the International Institute of Tropical Agriculture in Nigeria. In 1971, these institutes established the Consultative

Group on International Agricultural Research under the coordination of the president of the World Bank, Robert McNamara. Other research institutes were incorporated into this group, including the International Potato Center in Peru, the West African Rice Development Association in Liberia, the International Laboratory for Research on Animal Diseases in Kenya, the International Board for Plant Genetic Resources in Italy, the International Livestock Centre for Africa in Ethiopia, the International Food Policy Research Institute in the United States, the International Center for Agricultural Research in the Dry Areas in Syria and the International Service for National Agriculture Research in the Netherlands. These institutions received funding from governments, UN agencies and corporations such as Bayer, Chevron, Dow Chemical, Esso Engineering, Hoechst, Monsanto and Shell (Shiva 1991: 43).

One of the main private funders of these institutions was the Rockefeller Group, which also had a strong influence on Brazil's agricultural policy, as a letter from Alysson Paulinelli — the minister of agriculture during the Ernesto Geisel regime (1974–79) and the president of the Brazilian Confederation of Agriculture (Confederação Nacional da Agricultura) — demonstrates. In a letter addressed to Rodman C. Rockefeller, Minister Paulinelli thanked him for sending a speech Rockefeller had made during an Agribusiness Council meeting in 1975. He wrote, "I would like to thank you again for sending it so quickly and for your strong words of encouragement to convince investors to bring the benefits of their technology and capital to Brazil, thereby contributing to the development of Brazilian agriculture even further" (Rockefeller Foundation Archives 1976).[2]

The international promotion of industrial inputs for agriculture generated dependency in several countries. Shiva (1991) explained that prior to the adoption of this system, agricultural production in India was more abundant and diversified. Dependency on industrial supplies and monocropping reduce soil fertility and genetic diversity. Based on a demand that was artificially created among farmers in various countries, institutions such as the US Agency for International Development (USAID) and the World Bank designed special lines of financing for the purchase of chemical supplies, including fertilizers, pesticides and seeds, which many countries began to import. At the same time, these agencies promoted free trade policies (Shiva 1991: 30).

In the 1970s, the fertilizer sector was among the four largest industries in the world, coming in behind the oil, steel and cement. According to John W. Mellor, USAID chief economist at the time, "in general, the Green Revolution is mainly a fertilizer scheme" (Perelman 1979: 169). World Bank data from that decade showed that at least half of US fertilizer exports were subsidized by the government (Perelman 1979: 169–71). This policy became essential for perpetuating the United States' control over the world grain market and the dependency of other countries on "food aid" programs.

As with other agribusiness sectors, the seed corporations went through a process of mergers and acquisitions in the 1970s, when the market came mainly under the control of transnational petrochemical and pharmaceutical corporations, such as Monsanto, Pfizer, Shell and ARCO. Seeds took on a double role: they became a means of production and a commodity. They can be compared to the legendary phoenix, as they re-emerge from the ashes of the productive process in which they are consumed. The production of hybrid seeds, which do not naturally reproduce the parent plant the way that nonhybrid seeds do, constitutes a determining factor in the "opening of new frontiers for capital accumulation." The seed industry also required new legal instruments of intellectual property (Kloppenburg 1988: 10–11).

Exporting the Agribusiness System to Latin America

As part of his efforts to expand the agribusiness system internationally, Ray Goldberg published the 1974 book *Agribusiness Management for Developing Countries — Latin America*, in which he proposed a "conceptual model" to promote the production of commodities capable of meeting consumers' needs in the United States. He described the agribusiness system as the integration of corporations dealing with transportation, storage, commercialization and finance, while highlighting the role of a particular institution — the Latin American Agribusiness Development Corporation (LAAD) — in the coordination of this process:

> The agribusiness commodity system exists for the purpose of catering to the consumer's nutritional needs, his style of living, and his society's changing value structure. It encompasses all the participants in the production, processing, and marketing of a single farm product, including farm suppliers, farmers, storage operators, processors, wholesalers, and retailers involved in a commodity flow from initial inputs to the final consumer. It also includes all the institutions and arrangements that affect and coordinate the successive stages of a commodity flow, such as the government, markers, future markers, contractual integration, vertical integration, trade associations, cooperatives, corporate joint ventures, financial partners, financial entities, transport groups and educational organizations. (Goldberg 1974: 4)

Goldberg noted that the concept of agribusiness was widely accepted by the public and had been included in the strategic planning of governments and corporations and in academic courses of eighty universities in the United States and at least ten universities in other countries.

The book *Agribusiness in Latin America* by James Austin (1974) represents another example of the influence of US academia in the region. Austin was a professor at Harvard University's Central American Institute of Business Administration, where he was director of agribusiness programs. He also worked as a consultant for international agencies and various agribusiness corporations in Latin America. The book's preface, by Ray Goldberg, emphasized the idea that agribusiness expansion would solve the world's food shortage:

> The current global food scarcities and the concomitant rise in food prices demonstrate that in spite of the impressive progress made in agricultural technology in recent years, the world is not free from the treat of serious crop shortfalls.... In many of the developing countries, agricultural potential is being wasted because of the inability to bring more modern technology and management to bear on the problems of production, processing, storage, distribution, and marketing. The Agribusiness Council, a non-profit, membership organization of which I have the honor to serve as chairman, is dedicated to bringing the resources and capabilities of agribusiness firms to bear on economic development. (Austin 1974: 4)

Austin defined the term "agribusiness" as a system made up of three components: the first, or "operational," component consists of farmers, processing companies, warehousing and distribution companies; the second component includes input companies, credit banks and research institutes; and the third component consists of "coordinating" mechanisms, including governmental agencies, legal and contractual mechanisms, business associations and futures markets. Austin argued that the main economic activity in Latin American countries should be agribusiness for export. But during the initial expansion of the agribusiness system in the 1950s and 1960s, production in Latin America grew by only 1.9 percent, and 15 percent of all agricultural land in the region was used for the production of four commodities: coffee, sugar, bananas and cotton (Austin 1974: 4–6).

In 1985, the debut issue of *Agribusiness: An International Journal* recognized Davis and Goldberg as the first authors to define the concept of agribusiness and the first to create an academic course on the subject in 1956 at Harvard University. In the introduction, the editor suggested that the adoption of technological innovations in agriculture created new businesses for chemical inputs, since farmers had to buy almost all inputs from corporations.

The journal's introduction defined agribusiness as "the most important sector of the world's economy" and as a "global food system" that includes consumers, marketing, processing, agricultural and chemical companies, as well as "coordinating" institutions, such as government agencies, futures markets, structures to facilitate mergers and joint ventures, international trade agreements, research institutions, multilateral financial institutions (such as the World Bank) and transnational corporations. Within the international context, agribusiness is described as "an important sector of nearly every country's economy. As countries develop, the input supply industries and commodity processing, food manufacturing, and distribution firms tend to evolve and grow while the production sector shrinks in terms of number of people employed" (Woolverton 1985: 1–3).

LAAD provided political and ideological support to promote the agribusiness concept in the region. This institution was created during the Cold War, in the same period when the US government was implementing the Alliance for Progress project in Latin America to counter the influence of the United Nations' Economic Commission for Latin America and the Caribbean (ECLAC) and its director, Raul Prebisch: "Dr. Prebisch's arguments were thoroughly debated in Washington. In a masterful move designed to take the moral high ground away from the Cuban approach to development, President John F. Kennedy announced the Alliance for Progress in 1961" (Ross 2000: 11).

Robert Ross was president of LAAD from 1972 to 1998, but his influence on businesses and governments in Latin American countries predates this period. Through his relationship with ECLAC, in 1962 he became a professor at the UN Latin American and Caribbean Institute for Economic and Social Planning in Chile, and later he worked at the Central Bank of Paraguay. In 1965, Ross worked in Peru for the Adela Investment Company, formed by a group of multinational corporations interested in operating in Latin America (Ross 2000: xiv). The creation of LAAD in 1972 had the explicit objective of "strengthening private agribusiness companies in Latin America," but, according to Ross (2000: 12), "it is clear that the primary motivation for this massive aid program to Latin America was intended to stem the spread of Communist influence and to strengthen the overall security position of the United States and its allies."

Some of the major corporations that promoted LAAD were Cargill, Monsanto, Borden, Caterpillar Tractor Company, CPC International, Dow Chemical, Gerber Products, Ralston Purina, Standard Fruit and Steamship Company and Goodyear Tire and Rubber Company, as well as banks such as Rabobank Nederland, Chase Manhattan, Bank of America, Girard Bank and Southeast Banking Corporation of Miami. Similar institutions were created during the same period, such as Private Investment Company for Asia, based in Tokyo, and the International Society for Investment Finance in Africa, based in Geneva. LAAD's main office was in Panama because foreign corporations did not pay taxes there.

According to Ross, over three decades in Latin America, LAAD was successful in becoming a "profitable corporation specializing in financing investments in agribusiness projects." He was especially concerned about agrarian reform programs and governmental policies to control food prices in Chile, El Salvador, Peru and Bolivia:

> In all four countries, agricultural production stagnated as efficient farmers were chased off their land and replaced by poor and inefficient farmers. These new farmers were accustomed to produce for their own families and not for the market place. They are not bankable. They were illiterate and unable to learn new technologies. (Ross 2000: 14)

The idea that agrarian reform processes and peasant production methods were not "efficient" served to promote the role of multinational corporations in agriculture. The expansion of agribusiness in Latin America increased market concentration of machinery and chemical inputs. The tractor industry, for example, was controlled by four US corporations (Deere, International Harvester, Ford and J. I. Case) and one Canadian corporation, Massey Ferguson. In the 1970s, these companies set up subsidiaries in Latin America, especially in countries where agribusiness had more access to government incentives and low labour costs, such as Brazil, Mexico and Argentina (Burbach and Flynn 1980: 110–38). During the military dictatorships in Brazil, Argentina, Chile and Uruguay, wages decreased while the level of labour exploitation increased. Since the costs of chemical and industrial inputs were internationally standardized, Latin American countries sought to maintain acceptable levels of competitiveness through greater exploitation of rural workers.

Intensive use of chemical inputs in the agricultural system based on monocropping destroys biodiversity, causes soil erosion and loss of natural nutrients and pollutes water sources, affecting key elements for maintaining high productivity levels. Another impact is the development of resistance to certain types of pesticides in monocrop plantations, which leads to increases in the amount and types of chemicals used, as well as the levels of environmental destruction.

The largest fertilizer producers, which controlled the world market, started to operate in Latin America as part of the internationalization of agribusiness. These were US corporations, such as W. R. Grace, Monsanto, International Minerals & Chemical, Williams Companies, Beker Industries, Exxon and Allied Chemicals. Initially, these corporations prioritized the exportation of fertilizers to so-called Third World countries rather than creating subsidiaries for local production. The export of fertilizers was subsidized by the US government through USAID. The main markets in Latin America were Chile and Brazil. In the mid-1970s, fertilizer corporations started to set up subsidiaries in Latin American countries, taking advantage of subsidies from local governments and funding from multilateral financial institutions such as the Inter-American Development Bank (Burbach and Flynn 1980: 112–15). These corporations also benefited from access to low-cost energy sources and the lack of environmental regulations.

In the 1970s, the global market of pesticides was controlled by Dow Chemical, Eli Lilly, Dupont, Monsanto and Chevron. These corporations took advantage of the lack of environmental regulations in countries of the Global South by dumping several substances that had been prohibited in the United States, such as DDT (Burbach and Flynn 1980: 117). These products achieved widespread use, even among small farmers, as they were much cheaper compared to chemical fertilizers and machinery used more commonly in large plantations.

Production for both national markets and export in the region became concentrated in the hands of a few agribusiness corporations that had established subsidiaries in Latin America. This was the case, for example, of United Fruit, Swift and Armour and Cargill. Large banks such as Morgan Guaranty Trust and Chase Manhattan also operated in agricultural export markets. Regarding the role of Brazil, although the country is a major exporter of agricultural products, this trade has been mainly controlled by foreign corporations. Burbach and Flynn (1980: 131–34) observed that in the 1980s, Brazil was the second-largest exporter of agricultural commodities, after the United States, but national companies had a marginal role in international trade. For example, the Anderson Clayton corporation was the largest exporter of Brazilian cotton; orange juice from Brazil was exported by Minute Maid, a subsidiary of Coca-Cola; Cargill was the main exporter of soy and General Foods traded most Brazilian coffee. Monopolies over trade in certain sectors and the growing role of financial corporations stimulated speculation in agricultural commodities markets, including futures markets. By controlling global markets, large trading corporations were able to speculate on the price of agricultural commodities.

The history of these corporations reveals that the monopolization of agribusiness happened in the postwar period and its expansion in Latin America was facilitated by the military dictatorships in the 1960s. In the 1970s, five corporations owned by eight families dominated 85 percent of the global market of grains: Cargill, Continental Grain, Bunge, Dreyfus and Andre-Garnac. These groups controlled not only the market of agricultural commodities but also storage containers, transportation systems and port terminals for export. Despite their influence in various agribusiness sectors, these corporations preferred to control trade but not necessarily agricultural production because of the potential risks, for example, those related to weather conditions and economic instability. This explains why part of the production process is done by small and medium farmers who are expected to participate in the "production chains" of agribusiness.

A key mechanism for controlling international markets is operating in futures markets, which include speculation on the price of agricultural commodities and other aspects such as cargo space contracts and exchange rate markets. Speculation on cargo spaces influences the price of grains in international markets. For instance, the destination of shipments may change according to the perceived business advantages in certain countries, especially when food is scarce. This type of mechanism also allows trading corporations to speculate in foreign exchange markets, as they negotiate with currencies from different countries.

The global influence of agribusiness corporations stimulated land concentration and the expansion of monocropping of agricultural commodities. In this context, Latin American countries maintained a neocolonial role as suppliers of raw materials that respond to the demands of industrialized countries, even during times when the price of raw materials is on the decline and the price of imported industrial inputs is on the rise. Land concentration involves the expropriation of peasants' land, labour exploitation on large plantations and the appropriation of surplus labour of peasant production. This is the case in the *colonato* system, in which peasants cultivate a plot of land in exchange for a certain amount of labour or product surplus. Other forms of exploitation of peasant labour that agribusiness corporations use are supply contracts, which require peasant farmers to produce certain commodities, and land lease agreements that enable the corporations to expand the monocropping of commodities. These types of contracts frequently drive peasants into debt, even to the point where they may lose their land, as they assume all production risks and become vulnerable to fluctuations in commodity markets.

Especially since the 1960s, the expansion of agribusiness in Latin American countries has caused the displacement of rural communities and migration to urban centres, increasing unemployment and creating a contingent of expendable workers to maintain low wages. Despite the rural exodus, peasants and small farmers produce most of the food for local markets and have organized large grassroots movements for agrarian reform.

The Concept of Agribusiness in Brazil

In Brazil, the term "agribusiness" is used to justify the creation of "production chains" with the goal of incorporating data on agrochemical, industrial and trade activities into calculations of agriculture's contribution to the GDP. The monopoly of land and an agricultural policy geared towards the external market are not new in the country's history. Caio Prado Jr. (1970: 23) described the role of colonial Brazil as a "country-company" that supplied agricultural and mineral products to Europe:

> If we go back to the essence of our making, we will see that, in fact, we set ourselves up to supply sugar, tobacco and some other commodities; then, gold and diamonds; and then cotton and, soon after, coffee for European trade.... This beginning dominated Brazil's development for centuries and eventually became deeply and fully engraved in the features of and life in the country, especially its economic structure. And it continues to be this way even today.

Ever since colonial times, Brazil's economic policy has given priority to providing incentives for the export of agricultural and mineral commodities. The concept of agribusiness in Brazil is based on a perspective that sees development as a synonym of technological progress, which occurs in phases. This vision is present in the definition of "production chains." The Brazilian Agricultural Research Corporation (Embrapa) incorporated this approach in the 1990s to include "off the farm" sectors — such as chemical and industrial inputs, infrastructure and trading corporations — as clients. This strategy was based on the work of Davis and Goldberg. Initially, these activities were part of the so-called agroindustrial complex. The adoption of the term "agribusiness" was more recent (Castro, Lima and Cristo 2002: 6).

This system, as Favero (1996) put it, includes "both the concentration of power and the decentralization of productive tasks and services."

Decentralization is characterized by the implementation of "productive partnerships," in which "different actors organize themselves in a hierarchical manner ... that translates into relations of domination/subordination." In Favero's view, this subordination is positive because it allows for mass production by "increasing the capacity of certain actors to compete in an increasingly demanding and globalized market." According to this perspective, subordination would ensure "regularity" in world markets and "rigorous discipline of relations among industries and farmers" (Favero 1996: 279–302).

In Brazil, the essentially organic base of farming was gradually replaced by industrial inputs. While the industrial products used in agriculture represented 10 percent of production costs in 1949, this rate rose to 25 percent by the late 1960s and reached 40 percent in 1980. The greatest increase took place in 1965, when costs rose 7 percent in comparison to the previous year. The use of fertilizers showed annual growth of 13 percent between 1950 and 1985; between 1967 and 1980, this rate reached 17 percent a year (Kageyama 1987: 120–28). Until 1920, the only sector that had adopted some form of mechanization was the sugarcane industry. In 1940, mechanization was partially introduced in the production of coffee in the state of São Paulo and wheat and rice in Rio Grande do Sul. Large-scale mechanization was mainly adopted in the 1960s on soybean plantations, stimulated by subsidized credit. Three corporations — Massey Ferguson, Ford and Valmet — held a monopoly over the production of tractors, while combine manufacturing was controlled primarily by Massey, Schneider Logemann (SLC) and New Holland. The latter was later taken over by Ford (Kageyama 1987: 149–50).

The use of pesticides increased around the world during the postwar period, and these products began to be used more intensively in Brazil in 1961, when the Ministry of Agriculture eliminated import barriers on chemicals. Between 1974 and 1981, subsidized credit for these supplies grew 213 percent. This increase was proportionally higher than the 92 percent rise in the overall costs of agricultural production in the same period. The hike in oil prices had a significant impact on costs. In the 1980s, Brazil was the fourth-largest consumer of herbicides, fungicides and insecticides in the world, and the largest consumer of agrochemicals in Latin America (Kageyama 1987: 139–40). Today, Brazil continues to be one of the largest consumers of pesticides in the world.

Up until the 1970s, the global fertilizer market was controlled by transnational corporations with headquarters in the United States and Europe. In the 1980s, a series of mergers and joint ventures intensified the formation of a monopoly industry. In a period marked by the implementation of neoliberal policies, the Brazilian government disseminated the idea that both large landowners and peasant farmers should modernize their operations by adopting an agrarian program called New Rural World (Novo Mundo Rural). This program stimulated the privatization of public lands at the expense of an agrarian reform program. The World Bank promoted this concept by providing loans to the Brazilian government for the creation of the Ticket to Land (Cédula da Terra), Land Bank (Banco da Terra) and Land Credit (Crédito Fundiário) programs. Even though its strategy was rooted in neoliberal ideology that defended minimal state intervention, the World Bank demanded that the Brazilian government create a state fund to guarantee its projects, which compromised the budget for agrarian reform (Mendonça 2018).

The discourse on Brazil's "vocation" for agriculture, invoked to defend an economic model based on monocropping for exports, is used to ensure that agribusiness maintains its extensive nature through its alliance with the latifundium oligarchy. According to Delgado (2012: 2–4),

> In the current context, the reasons for the success of several "sectors" that are growing more than others — agriculture, mining, hydroelectricity and oil exploration — are derived from a set of external economic conditions that highlight natural comparative advantages and the appropriation of land income as the main drivers of capital accumulation in the Brazilian economic system.

Despite the predominance of the agroexport model, up until the 1970s the Brazilian state played a significant role in the management of food stocks by establishing export quotas and controls on agricultural imports. During that period, the policy of providing state support for food production sought to respond, to a certain extent, to the needs of the domestic market. It also subsidized the reproduction of the labour force with low wages in industrial sectors by keeping food prices low (Mendonça 2018).

The end of the military dictatorship in Brazil coincided with the dissemination of a discourse that defended fiscal "austerity" and "free" trade policies. Neoliberal reforms were presented as the solution to the external debt crisis. The 1990s were marked by the privatization of state enterprises and the deregulation of food stocks. Social demands for agrarian reform were not heeded and, as a result, the rural exodus process intensified and contributed to the so-called urbanization of poverty. In this so-called new economic order, the increasing concentration of private capital was stimulated by joint ventures that intensified the formation of monopolies in different economic sectors, including agribusiness. The constitution of private monopolies with control over agricultural production and trade happened while financial capital was gaining predominance in agriculture with the strengthening of futures markets and other financial mechanisms.

The provision of subsidized credit and the frequent rollover of agribusiness's debts were coordinated with the adoption of free trade policies to consolidate the sector's advantages based on monocropping for exports. One example was the approval of the Kandir Law, which enabled the government to create new types of tax incentives for agricultural exports from 1996 on. Even with this measure, the problem of indebtedness in the agribusiness sector remained. In 1999, the government forgave US$18 billion of the sector's debt; the trade surplus announced for that year totalled US$10 billion. Agribusiness's product, then, is debt itself (Mendonça 2018).

In recent years, farmland in Brazil has been the target of speculation by financial institutions, particularly international pension funds, which has caused major increases in land prices. These increases have been stimulated by the partnerships established between the large landowning oligarchy and transnational financial and agribusiness corporations.[3]

The Influence of "Evolutionary Economics" on the Concept of Agribusiness

In *A Concept of Agribusiness*, Davis and Goldberg acknowledged the influence of Kenneth E. Boulding's "evolutionary economics" in their defence of agribusiness development. Boulding applied biological mechanisms to define economic tendencies and saw development as a result of technological progress. His theory is based on the idea that "progress" and "development" are linear processes driven by the creation of new technologies. He projected an image of a supposed civilized world related to urban life: "The superior power of scientific images usually ensures the triumph of the scientific image over the competing folk image, but nevertheless the struggle may be long and painful" (Boulding 1964: 56–57).

According to this view, technological development has the capacity to generate universal benefits. To justify factors such as poverty and inequality, Boulding (1964: 226) pointed to "difficulties with economic development in poor countries" and population growth:

> This is due mainly to the very rapid growth in the population of the cities, sometimes because of refugees from war or from the

relocation of frontiers, and almost always because of the rapid population increase in rural areas that forces people out of these areas into the cities, simply because the rural economy is only adjusted to a fairly constant labour force.

This type of doctrine even blamed improvements in children's health for economic problems:

> One of the most difficult problems facing mankind in the present historical era is the control of its own population.... A sudden improvement in the health of the people and especially in the health of children could prove to be a disaster.... When there is a very large population of children and young people, it becomes increasingly difficult to provide the resources for the kind of education which is necessary if society is to pass over into the modern world. (Boulding 1964: 121–23)

Boulding's ideas influenced Davis, who saw the transformation of agriculture into "business" as an evolutionary and inevitable process caused by ongoing technological improvement:

> In general, the spokesmen for major economic interests — including farm leaders, businessmen, public officials, and even professional experts — have been slow to comprehend the magnitude of the evolutionary forces which are converting *agriculture* into *agribusiness* and *farm problems* into *business problems*. They have been slow to recognize the inevitability of the changes which are inherent in the application of improved technology — changes in such factors as the size of unit, organization, managerial competence, technical skills, capital requirements, and market potentials. (Davis and Hinshaw 1957: 1)

The idea of development as a linear process of technological evolution continued to be disseminated by the promoters of agribusiness. The recognition of factors that indicate the permanence of a crisis in relation to the expansion of agribusiness also recurred in the analysis of several authors, including Davis and Goldberg. They explained this crisis as a natural consequence of the industrialization of agriculture, instead of analyzing it from a critical perspective. The industrialization of agriculture generates a disproportional increase in constant capital in relation to variable capital or the possibility of exploiting surplus value. Market concentration is a key piece of this process since it eliminates competition as a driving force for the development of productive forces.

This dynamic explains the continuing crisis in the expansion of agribusiness corporations, which depend on subsidized credit and other forms of state support:

> The total value of farmers' marketing has stayed about the same for several years, but as the number of farmers has decreased, sales per capita have increased. That is, the same pie is divided among fewer people. This is a good trend, because it means that per capita farm incomes are trying to keep pace with higher per capita incomes in non-farming occupations. Even the amount of hired labour used for seasonable farm work is declining as farmers substitute machines for hand-labour. Another factor in farmers' income is the increasing size of federal payments under various agricultural programs, which have the effect of stabilizing farm income. (Roy 1967: 12–13)

The increasing mechanization of agriculture in the United States between 1910 and 1960 was inversely proportional to the use of labour, while the cultivated area did not expand:

> When we consider land, labour and capital as the prime factors in farm inputs, it is evident that *land* remains constant. Its contribution is about 8.5 per cent of the total. *Labor*, on the other hand, has dropped by more than a half, contributing about 30 per cent at present, compared with 75 percent in 1910. *Capital* items (buildings, livestock, machinery, equipment, credit funds, etc.) have about quadrupled, contributing 61 per cent at present, compared with only 17 per cent in 1910.... An increase in farm technology puts more emphasis on specialization and research findings rather than on farmer-discovered technology. (Roy 1967: 25–26)

During the nineteenth century, mechanical technologies were introduced to increase labour productivity in US agriculture. In the twentieth century, the main changes occurred in relation to biological and chemical techniques introduced into agriculture, especially from 1930 on. World War I generated a larger demand for grain exports from the United States to Europe, which led to a sharp rise in food prices, which nearly doubled between 1916 and 1920. That period was also marked by speculation on the price of farmland, which rose by 70 percent between 1913 and 1920.

However, in the mid-1920s, this trend reversed, and food prices fell by about 50 percent, generating a widespread crisis among farmers who could not repay their real estate debts. This crisis in agriculture preceded the Great Depression, leading to the collapse of financial markets and the recession in industrial sectors that culminated in 1929. During that period, the productivity in US agriculture remained stable, but farmers' incomes fell by 50 percent (Cochrane 1993: 100–101).

Changes in production patterns — namely, the growing dependency on industrial inputs in agriculture — intensified in the 1950s, after World War II. These technologies were initially developed by the USDA and later appropriated by private corporations as the basis of the so-called agribusiness complex. A main stimulus to the industrialization of agriculture was the creation of gasoline engines for tractors in 1901, which allowed for their use on a large scale. In 1911, the estimated number of tractors in the United States was 4,000. This number multiplied in subsequent decades to 264,000 in 1920 and 920,000 in 1930. Between 1910 and 1930, the use of nitrogen-based fertilizers increased by 60 percent. However, agricultural productivity only increased 9 percent between 1910 and 1920 and 15 percent between 1920 and 1930. During the following decades, massive use of chemical inputs and mechanization in agriculture was facilitated by access to credit and subsidies. In 1940, the number of tractors in the United States was estimated at 1.6 million. This number increased to 3.4 million in 1950 and to 4.7 million in 1960. The use of nitrogen-based fertilizers increased from 419 million tons in 1940 to 7,459 million tons in 1970, and potassium-based inputs grew from 435 million tons in 1940 to 4,035 million tons in 1970 (Cochrane 1993: 108–26).

In 1938, the US Congress approved the Agricultural Adjustment Act, creating new mechanisms for providing governmental support to farmers, especially to finance a soil conservation policy. This program also included price guarantees for certain agricultural products, established market quotas to prevent overproduction of certain commodities and increased funding for food stamps for low-income families and food purchases by public schools. Despite these measures, agricultural overproduction persisted, and the US Congress expanded incentives to facilitate grain exports, such as authorizing payment in importing countries' currencies instead of in US dollars. The standardization of food production was expanded in the 1970s during the global economic crisis, when the price of commodities, including oil and agricultural products, increased in international markets. This crisis of overproduction in the United States is described by agribusiness promoters as "that old farm problem, abundance, [which] continued to be a plague on American agriculture, having escaped all the remedies that have been tried over the many years since World War II" (Hampe, Witteberg and Edds 1980: 79).

The 1967 book *Exploring Agribusiness* by Ewell Paul Roy was used to disseminate the agribusiness concept in academic spaces. It shows how farmers became dependent on chemical inputs, which replaced organic inputs previously developed and produced on the farms. Other activities that were formerly done on the farms, such as storage, processing and distribution of food and fibre, were transferred to large corporations. The greatest concentration of capital in agribusiness started in the packaging industry, especially in the canned, glass, tube and paper sectors, as well as in the fertilizer, tire and oil refining industries: "The present agribusiness economy has come about by the gradual dispersion of functions *from* agriculture *to* business" (Roy 1967: 41–42).

Data from the 1960s show that the amount of steel used on US farms was equivalent to the amount used to produce five million compact cars, and the amount of rubber was more than what was needed to produce tires for six million cars. At that time, oil consumption by agribusiness was higher than in any other industrial sector in the United States, reaching fifteen billion barrels per year, which demanded special credit lines subsidized by the government (Roy 1967: 11). The production of chemical inputs in the United States increased 172 percent between 1960 and 1976. The largest pesticide and fertilizer corporations were closely linked to oil and mining industries. The main groups controlling the production of chemical inputs were Ciba-Geigy, Monsanto, Elanco, Allied Chemicals, Phillips Petroleum Company, International Minerals & Chemical, Dow Chemical and CF Industries (Rawlins 1980: 68–81).

In the 1960s, 20 percent of the United States' territory was used for agriculture, while 28 percent was used for pasture, 34 percent was covered by forests and the remaining 18 percent was used for other purposes. As a result of the postwar crisis of overproduction, thirty million acres of agricultural land were converted back into forests and pastures. The government turned public lands, which account for about one-third of the country, into protected areas to conserve forests, to preserve soil fertility, moisture and rivers, and to prevent flooding and other natural disasters. Approximately 400 million acres were used for agriculture. According to the US agricultural census of 1960, one-third of the approximately 3.9 million farms in the country were considered family owned, despite the growing concentration of land in large farms. On family farms, at least 50 percent of the work was done by family members, and their production represented 70 percent of the agricultural market, compared with 66 percent in 1944. Only 150,000 farms were considered large properties (Roy 1967: 43–45). These farms became more specialized and less diversified to meet the demands of the agribusiness monocropping system.

In *Agricultural Economics and Agribusiness*, Gail L. Cramer, Clarence W. Jensen, and Douglas DeWitt Southgate (2001: 9) defined agribusiness as "the sum total of all operations involved in the manufacture and distribution of farm supplies; production operations on the farm; and the storage, processing and distribution of farm commodities and items made from them." As a theoretical reference, the authors used Thomas Malthus's principle of population, according to which population growth would lead humanity to a catastrophic stage due to the impossibility of increasing food production proportionately. The myth of food shortages was used to justify the expansion of US agricultural exports and the policy of price guarantees for agribusiness corporations through dumping and subsidies:

> Because of the excess capacity in the United States, the export market has been important for the agricultural sector. In the past, the export market has been a place to dump surplus production, but with the recent changes in the demand for agricultural commodities, it appears that agribusiness firms will have an opportunity to sell more of their output in foreign markets. This market is especially relevant if world-wide food shortages continue to exist and production controls on US agriculture are not needed to maintain farm income. (Cramer, Jensen and Southgate 2001: 455)

Agribusiness promoters advocated for expanding the use of land, machinery, fertilizers and pesticides, identifying a growing monopolization of the chemical input, distribution and marketing sectors by large corporations. An estimated 50 percent of all corporate assets in the United States would be concentrated in the agribusiness sector, which includes chemical inputs, transportation and distribution corporations, credit institutions, supermarket chains, restaurants and small farmers. Despite the process of land concentration, in 1987 family farmers represented 87 percent of farms in the United States (Cramer, Jensen and Southgate 2001: 24). The main change was the process of "integrating" family farmers with agribusiness corporations through "specialization" or the standardization of agriculture that prioritized the monocropping of commodities. Land concentration is seen in the decrease in the number of farms, from 6.8 million in 1935 to about 3 million in 1970, on the same amount of cultivated land (Cochrane 1993:

132–33). In 1976, this number was 2.8 million, representing a 30 percent decrease from the 3.9 million farms recorded in the US agricultural census of 1960. The opposite trend was registered in the average size of farms, which rose from 297 acres in 1960 to 389 acres in 1976 (Rawlins 1980: 37).

The expansion of agribusiness increased market concentration, as well as the need to access larger amounts of credit, generating debt in a process of "substitution of labour for capital":

> One of the major changes occurring in farming during recent years has been the substitution of capital for labor. Around 1900, capital (including land) contributed about 25 percent to the production process, and labour accounted for 75 percent. Currently, about 70 percent of the production of food and fiber is attributed to capital, while labour only accounts for 30 percent.... As a result of increasing borrowing, interest payments have been one of the fastest-growing costs of farming. The index of prices paid by farmers for interest rose from 32 in 1956 to 302 in 1970.... USDA reports estimate that total farm debt now exceeds $100 billion, which represents an increase of more than 300 percent since 1960. (Rawlins 1980: 87)

The internationalization of agribusiness was expanded by the dissemination of hybrid seeds developed by Nelson Borlaug, known as the father of the so-called green revolution, who was awarded the Nobel Peace Prize in 1970. Cultivation of this type of seed required a "technological package" based on chemical fertilizers and pesticides. The agribusiness system was presented as a solution to world hunger, and technological "progress" was promoted as a way to deal with crises in agriculture. But the negative impacts of these technologies, including machinery, chemical and biotechnology industries, became more evident especially after the 1980s, as indicated in the following statement:

> The value of DDT as an insecticide was discovered in 1939 by Dr. Paul Müller for which he received the 1948 Nobel Prize in Physiology and Medicine. DDT was the major compound used to control malaria mosquitoes during World War II, and the effectiveness of this compound encouraged researchers to develop other similar compounds as ... valuable insecticides. Ironically, many of the most successful pesticides which provided so much promise in earlier years have become enemies of the environment....

Numerous others will likely be declared illegal in the near future. (Rawlins 1980: 69)

Neo-Malthusian theory tries to explain world hunger as a consequence of population growth, ignoring key factors such as market speculation on agricultural commodities and the rising production costs of industrial agriculture, which demand oil-based inputs. The same type of ideology promoted forced sterilization of women in Latin America, Africa and Asia.

The promotion of agribusiness increased standardization of crops and land concentration worldwide; peasants were dispossessed of land as agribusiness sought to control farmland and rural labour. In the Global South, these policies generated dependency on chemical inputs and marketing channels controlled by large corporations. Replacing natural-based techniques with chemical inputs was a key factor in creating new possibilities for capital accumulation in industrial sectors that were able to transfer value from agriculture:

> Despite problems of perish-ability, agricultural commodities, once harvested, closely resemble other raw materials used as industrial inputs. Industrial processing operations often grew out of the trading activities of merchant capitals, as in the case of wheat and flour.… That is, unable to subsume the rural production *in toto*, selected rural activities have become sectors of accumulation for different fractions of industrial capital. (Goodman et al. 1987: 6–7)

The food processing industry uses agricultural raw materials as well as chemical and synthetic materials produced by pharmaceutical and petrochemical corporations. The commercialization of new brands of processed food requires large investments in advertising to create "product differentiation." This process favours promotion and advertising contracts for certain brands. Monopolies established in the processing and distribution sectors also contribute to capital concentration in retail, as in the case of supermarkets, which also create their own product brands through mergers and special contracts with suppliers. Large supermarkets, convenience stores and fast-food restaurants expanded their markets internationally as part of the agribusiness system.

A key concept for advancing the internationalization of agribusiness was the "green revolution," which included political, economic and technological elements. Its origins can be traced to the period of economic depression in the 1930s, when the US government adopted measures to restrict food imports and protect local agriculture. These policies included subsidies and price guarantees for food production, which generated a surplus of grain. The government financed exports and used "food aid" programs as a dumping strategy in international markets, generating dependency and destroying local agriculture in many countries. Especially from 1970 on, US agribusiness corporations intensified capital exports by establishing subsidiaries in several countries to produce chemical inputs as part of the "technological package" of the green revolution. These corporations also benefited from exchange rate deregulation, neoliberal trade policies and the increasing role of financial capital in agriculture.

The green revolution was initially promoted by private institutions, such as the Ford and Rockefeller foundations, in collaboration with USAID and the World Bank. In 1960, the Ford Foundation created the Intensive Agricultural Development Programme with the idea that natural resources in agriculture were underutilized. During the 1960s and 1970s, the Ford and Rockefeller foundations supported International Agricultural Research Centers to train agribusiness promoters in several countries and grant scholarships to foreign academics so they could study in US institutions. The green revolution was based on a claim of scientific neutrality to avoid criticism and justify corporate control over local agricultural systems. It also represented a power struggle in terms of what is considered legitimate scientific production: "While science itself is a product of social forces and has a social agenda determined by those who can mobilize scientific production, in contemporary times scientific activity has been assigned a privileged epistemological position of being socially and politically neutral" (Shiva 1991: 21–35).

The international promotion of the green revolution required certain ideological elements such as the claim that this production system was based on universally recognized technological advances, which would supposedly increase food productivity through, for example, the use of machinery and chemical inputs and the intensive use of water and energy. Strategies for implementing the green revolution included state policies that compelled peasants to produce certain crops and use chemical inputs such as pesticides and fertilizers, which benefited large corporations in that industrial sector. This type of policy promoted the extension of monocrop plantations and increased market monopolies of industrial inputs in agriculture. The impacts were land concentration, environmental destruction and higher exploitation of the labour force, as well as increasing poverty, hunger and migration of peasants to urban areas.

The green revolution promoted the internationalization of the agribusiness system, including the mechanization of farms and the use of chemical inputs. A strategy to support the use of these technologies was to generate dependency on industrial inputs, as well as fear of food scarcity. But food scarcity was aggravated by the expansion of monocrop plantations, destroying biodiversity and causing reductions in soil fertility and a significant change in farmland use in several countries.

This historical analysis is relevant today, as the agribusiness system continues to be associated with the image of "progress" and "technological evolution," despite the fact that industrial agriculture constitutes a main cause of climate change and the pollution of water sources. Agribusiness plantations demand the use of inputs based of fossil fuels, such as nitrogen-based fertilizers that destroy natural nutrients and reduce soil porosity and the availability of oxygen. This type of market generates political instability in a context of geopolitical disputes over oil and natural gas, as well as economic vulnerability caused by the role that these commodities play in the speculative movement of financial markets, as the following chapters demonstrate.

Notes

1. A 2001 biography of Ray Goldberg says, "Dr. Goldberg has served as an officer and director of numerous agribusiness films in the food and financial sectors of agriculture, and has been a consultant to a diverse group of public and private agencies including the Commodity Futures Trading Commission, Agency for International Development, President's Food and Fiber Commission, the National Marine Fisheries Service, US Comptroller of the Currency, National Academy of Sciences, World Food System Inc., Ford Foundation, Winrock International, institutes in Nicaragua and Mexico, and many other agriculturally oriented organizations. In addition, he is on the Editorial Board of the *Food Policy Journal* and similarly served for the *American Journal of Agricultural Economics*. About 150 Harvard M.B.A.s each year concentrate on an agribusiness major under Professor Goldberg's supervision. He directs the national and international agribusiness Continuing Education programs at the Harvard Business School. These programs bring together about 150 of the world's agribusiness leaders each year from private industry to analyze case studies of agribusiness production, marketing, and financial situations" (Cramer, Jensen and Southgate 2001: 3).
2. I would like to thank Clifford Andrew Welch for providing me with a copy of this document.
3. Several publications on this issue can be found on the website of Rede Social de Justiça e Direitos Humanos: <social.org.br>. See, for example, Pitta, Cerdas and Mendonça (2018).

2 Land as a Mechanism of Financial Accumulation

L and is a central element in the economic and geopolitical analysis of agribusiness. The historical investigation into the expansion of this agricultural system, presented in the first chapter of this book, required an understanding of theoretical categories of classical political economy. The history and political economy of agribusiness reveal current dynamics, for example, about how farmland represents a key asset in financial markets, as well as the interconnection between agriculture and energy markets, as described in the ensuing chapters of this book. The processes highlighted in these chapters are based on original research and fieldwork in Brazil, but they also represent a global pattern that becomes clearer when presented within a theoretical context, as in the case of land rent theory.

A central category of analysis concerning the role of agriculture in the capitalist mode of production is land rent. Marx's land rent theory is based on the understanding of capital as a set of social relations mediated by the commodity form and analyzed using the dialectical materialist method, which identifies economic trends from historical material conditions. The commodity form functions as a representation of abstract labour, and it is expressed by the apparently concrete nature of capitalist relations. Marx explained labour relations as concrete abstractions based on the dialectical connection between use value and exchange value.

The dialectical relation between essence and appearance, or abstract and concrete, is key to understanding the concept of commodity fetishism. Marx's theory of value and surplus value is based on capital-labour relations, even if labour is expressed through its negative form: the absence of labour. For Marx, human labour is a concrete abstraction—"expenditure of brain, nerves, muscles, senses" (1977, vol. 1: 13), which is the source of value in the commodity form, based on the contradiction between use value and exchange value. Fetishism hides the essence or the source of value, which is labour social time. Exchange value is a result of the abstraction of use values in the commodity form that objectifies labour. Exchange value becomes apparent in its fetishist form expressed in the price of commodities, which hides abstract labour as the source of value. Marx described the secret of commodities as the way in which average social labour time constitutes value. The individual labour time of workers is diluted into social labour time, and so time becomes a simultaneous concept instead of a linear process.

Following this logic, a change in productive forces is not necessarily a linear successive development, as it is explained in positivist interpretations. Instead, it reveals a dialectical social relation in which time can be interpreted as a simultaneous concept and space as an abstraction. The contradiction in the organic composition of capital (constant and variable) is not a result of a mechanical or linear process of increasing "development" or technological change. The development of productive forces increases the proportion of constant capital or "dead" labour (machinery, infrastructure, raw materials, technology, etc.) in the organic composition of capital in relation to variable capital ("living" labour). One result is what Marx described as disposable-labour time, which generates a contradiction in capitalist relations that consider labour as the source of value.

The dialectical materialist method serves as a basis for understanding the theory of the tendency of the profit rate to fall in industrial sectors and the tendency of land rent to decrease in agriculture. This analysis includes the dialectical relation between accumulation and crisis as simultaneous and permanent elements in the logic of capital, even if they appear in a polarized and cyclical way. In other words, crisis is accumulation, and accumulation is crisis.

Land rent presupposes a special monopoly over "a portion of the globe" (Marx 1985, vol. 3) that is appropriated as private property. Some key elements for increasing land rent include specific natural conditions or productive forces that are not the result of human labour, such as soil fertility, water sources and biodiversity. Private property of land and its natural resources enables capital reproduction through the appropriation of abstract labour converted into land rent. Natural productive forces increase labour productivity but cannot be reproduced by human labour, and so private property of land is always monopoly property. For example, a piece of land with water sources requires less capital investment to reach a certain level of labour productivity than land that requires irrigation systems. Of course, natural resources constitute key elements of use value that benefit society as a whole when they are not exploited as a source of exchange value.

The role of private property is historically constructed, considering the multiple forms of land use and land tenure. In Brazil, the legal framework for a land market began in 1850 with a colonial law that consolidated private property of land based on negotiable titles, which are abstractions in comparison with land use based on occupation and cultivation by the diversity of peasant and Indigenous communities, who demonstrate multiple forms of territorial organization (Paoliello 1992: 4–5). Of course, the institution of private property is not particular to agriculture. Like other categorical forms in capitalist social relations, such as labour and value, private property determines this mode of production. However, a monopoly over land has specific roles as a result of the "relative rarity of the land factor" (Vergopoulos 1977: 57–58).

The "land factor" is a productive force that cannot be reproduced by human labour but has the capacity to increase labour productivity. Productive forces such as soil fertility, water sources, biodiversity and other elements of differential land rent can also function to minimize contradictions in the organic composition of capital or in the relation between constant and variable capital. Differential land rent is a result of the "metamorphosis" of abstract labour into surplus labour, based on the difference between the average profit rate and the rate of profit generated in less productive soils that require larger capital investments to reach the average profit rate (Marx 1985, vol. 3). It also depends on location, considering the cost of transportation and commercialization of agriculture products, and on privileged access to credit and subsidies for production and marketing.

These elements of land rent are central to understanding current dynamics of the crisis of overaccumulation. The expansion of plantations by agribusiness requires larger investments in industrial inputs, transportation and commercialization of commodities. Through this process, land rent tends to decrease since larger capital investments are usually made in the most fertile soils, eliminating less productive properties from the regulating market of the average profit rate and, consequently, decreasing the profitability of the most productive properties.

An increase in the cost of production and labour productivity tends to cause the average land rent to decrease. Therefore, a crisis of overproduction is not a result of abundance of commodities and lack of consumer markets. In other words, it is not a simple matter of supply and demand. A crisis of overproduction or overaccumulation results because the development of productive forces decreases value. The increasing price of agricultural commodities does not "imply an increase in value, since only live labour creates value. Land ownership is a mechanism that allows value to be captured from labor" (Vergopoulos 1977: 58).

The agribusiness system intensifies dependency on industrial inputs and territorial expansion of plantations because of the destructive impacts of monocropping on natural resources. The reduction of profit rates in industrial sectors causes capital to "migrate" to less productive sectors such as agriculture to obtain higher-than-average profits. Due to its monopolistic characteristic, land rent generates special production conditions that allow value to be transferred to industrial sectors that have a higher organic composition. At the same time, elements of differential land rent, as well as large agribusiness corporations' privileged access to credit and subsidies, stimulate the overaccumulation of capital in agriculture. But this process of overaccumulation also generates crises, especially given the key role of financial capital in agricultural commodity markets.

The Peasant Economy

The historical process of transition from feudalism to capitalism was described by Marx as the "so-called primitive accumulation" (Marx 1983, vol. 1). Instead of describing this process as natural or mechanical, he looked at how institutionalized violence against peasants in Europe created new forms of labour exploitation in industrial sectors. When peasants were displaced from their land and lost their means of subsistence, they were forced to work in factories under conditions similar to slavery. The main categories of capitalist relations — abstract labour and value — were formed by the abrupt imposition of systematic policies of land expropriation from peasants, who were subjected to various forms of cruelty and torture or sentenced to death if they refused to work in factories. Another key element in the expansion of capitalism was colonization in other parts of the world. Based on this analysis, Marx concluded that all capitalist labour relations are forms of slave labour.

In the book *The Agrarian Question*, originally published in 1899, Kautsky (1968) presented a positivist view about the transition from feudalism to capitalism, considering the key role of small farmers in some contexts but mainly defending large agricultural production as a way to organize labour and gain access to raw materials, machinery and technology. Kautsky imagined that extensive agriculture based on plantations controlled by the state would eventually eliminate private ownership of farmland. For him, peasants represented a class in transition between the two main classes in capitalism: the proletarian and the bourgeoisie.

Kautsky's position underestimated the significant role of peasants in Europe during that period. In France and Germany, most of the agricultural production was done on the land of small peasant farmers. In Prussia, medium-sized production prevailed, and in some regions of Spain, semi-feudal latifundia still existed. At that time, large-scale, capitalist agricultural production was only developing in England (Hobsbawm 1984: 154). In his analysis of primitive accumulation and the expropriation of peasants during the transition from feudalism to capitalism, Marx clarified that he was referring to the particular situation in England: "The history of this expropriation assumes different aspects in different countries and runs through its various phases in different orders of succession and at different historical epochs. Only in England, which we therefore take as our example, has it the classic form" (Marx 1977, vol. 1: 876).

Eric Hobsbawm (1984) outlined classic Marxist debates on the socialist agrarian program based on different views on the effectiveness of capital concentration in agriculture versus peasant production. This discussion was guided by opposing interpretations of the supposed necessary succession of modes of production as a theoretical interpretation of the historical process. These perspectives became influential in other countries, even though they were based on a particular process of transition from feudalism to capitalism in the European context.

Rosa Luxemburg (1985) identified the role of noncapitalist production relations within the process of capital reproduction on a global scale. She analyzed internal contradictions of capital reproduction and accumulation, arguing against a linear, mechanical and deterministic interpretation of the development of productive forces. In addition to questioning the process of accumulation, Luxemburg inspired a methodological discussion about historical materialism and dialectics.

Leandro Konder (2009) criticized the positivist method in his book *The Defeat of Dialectics*. He used the concept of praxis to analyze the double role of human labour as an abstraction (alienation) in the production process and as a potential generator of critical and creative consciousness. Based on dialectical materialism, Konder questioned the idea of "evolutionary continuity" and the "rigid causality" of positivist thought.

The concept of praxis relates to Marx's theory of value, which considers subjectivity and objectivity in a simultaneous and dialectical relation, or the concept of labour as a concrete abstraction. In other words, both the empiricist notion that sees people as "spectators" of historical processes and the utopian view that imagines individuals as "conductors" of history are based on a common interpretation of the separation between subjectivity and objectivity.

Samir Amin (1977: 16) explained that "empiricism grasps capital based on immediately perceptible phenomena: the equipment in which it crystallizes, production in separate units where the equipment is located. The conventional economy's habit of starting from 'microeconomics' simply reflects its inability to understand that the totality is greater than the sum of its parts." For Lukács (2003: 117), the dialectical method always considers the totality of the historical process.

The concept of totality in opposition to fragmenting knowledge is also central to Henri Lefebvre's (2008: 181) work:

> When we try to particularize knowledge, we destroy it from within.... If there is no insistence upon totality, theory and practice accept the 'real' just as it is, and 'things' just as they are: fragmentary, divided and disconnected. Activities, and therefore individuals, become "reified" like things, and, just like things, are separated one from the other.

Marx developed the critique of empiricism and idealism in *Capital: A Critique of Political Economy.* He used the idealized character of Robinson Crusoe as an analogy to explain the dialectical relation of subjectivity and objectivity, since human labour is converted into a commodity in capitalist social relations.

The critique of positivism and idealism applies to the study of capitalist agriculture, which is often associated with the notion of development in international geopolitical contexts. The international division of labour establishes different roles for national economies in foreign relations. The development theory generates the impression that peripheral countries could develop their productive forces to reach a supposed ideal level, overlooking contradictions in this process. In considering the historical role of colonialism as a key element of primitive accumulation and the expansion of capitalism, it is clear that peripheral countries were central to the production and reproduction of capital; therefore, the "periphery" is as modern as the "centre" of capitalism.

Marx's original description of primitive accumulation was the basis for other authors to identify such mechanisms as permanent in the logic of capital reproduction. For Vergopoulos (1977: 48), "primitive accumulation does not only belong to prehistory or the history of capitalism, but it is also an indispensable assumption for the current daily renewal of the system."

This analysis explains the permanence of a significant portion of agricultural production that is not typically capitalist because it is not based on wage labour. However, considering the capitalist mode of production as a totality, peasant production is not external to capitalism. The portion of agricultural production that is not based on wage labour demands a larger workforce; therefore, it would not be viable in an extensive industrialized monocropping system. The definition of a peasant economy, typically noncapitalist but related in a contradictory way to the capitalist mode of production, conceives capital as a set of social relations. Peasants produce food for subsistence and have different forms of market relations, contributing to a large portion of diversified food production for local markets.

The fundamental categories of capitalist social relations — labour, land and capital — can also be used to describe the so-called peasant economic unity. In peasant production, the organization of labour as a specific "production unit" is usually more diverse than the traditional concept of a nuclear family unit. It is precisely the different form of labour organization that constitutes a central point in the debate about peasant agriculture.

Alexander V. Chayanov (1974) created the concept of "economic peasant unit" in the first few years after the Russian Revolution of 1917, when peasants represented 85 percent of the population in Russia. Both Marx and Chayanov identified that a portion of peasants' production surplus is donated to other social sectors. Marx explained the "genesis of capitalist land rent" (Marx 1985, vol. 3) as a portion of peasants' surplus labour that was given to society and was not calculated in the regulation of production prices. Chayanov (1974: 11) observed that peasants in Russia increased production when the price of food decreased, which is typically a noncapitalist response because corporations usually reduce production when prices fall.

A peasant economy is usually based on noncapitalist characteristics, but it is not isolated from capitalist social relations. Historically, peasant labour has included nonagricultural activities such as the manufacturing of house utensils and production tools. In certain situations, peasants also worked on plantations and in industrial sectors, and served in the army. Chayanov explained the diverse forms of labour organization in peasant units as an economic strategy for survival, but he did not intend to predict the future of peasant organizations.

In today's peasant economy, there continues to be a diversity of strategies and systems of production. For example, peasants sometimes combine food production for subsistence, participation in local markets and the sale of their labour force. Some peasant units also hire labour when necessary. The type of cultivation prioritized by peasants is also diverse and can combine subsistence farming with the production of certain crops within the agribusiness system. It is important to recognize the economic role of peasant agriculture, whether for local markets or for subsistence, which is commonly underestimated or even ignored in official economic data even though it provides food for the majority of the world's population. Currently, peasants and small farmers produce more than 70 percent of food worldwide, and about 3.5 billion people live in rural areas:

> There are 1.5 billion on 380 million farms; 800 million more growing urban gardens; 410 million gathering the hidden harvest of our forests and savannas; 190 million pastoralists and well over 100 million peasant fishers. At least 370 million of these are also Indigenous Peoples. Together these peasants make up almost half the world's peoples and they grow at least 70% of the world's food. (ETC Group 2009: 1)

Women peasants and farmworkers play a key role in food production for subsistence and for local markets, as they produce more than 50 percent of the world's food. Yet they own less than 2 percent of farmland (Monsalve Suárez 2015). For women in rural communities, the main challenge to achieving food sovereignty is control over economic resources and access to land.

Expansion of monocropping on agricultural commodity plantations intensifies the displacement of peasant and Indigenous communities. Financial and agribusiness corporations, as well as a number of countries, are pursuing the acquisition of farmland around the globe while farming and pastoral systems that produce food for local markets are being destroyed, causing a profound impact on climate change. The expansion of agribusiness also causes the pollution of water sources and the destruction of biodiversity, decreasing the level of productivity in agriculture and generating new destructive cycles of monocropping expansion to exploit natural resources. Armed conflicts, militarization and the repression of rural communities frequently involve control over land, water and mining resources. The monopoly of land property blocks the creation of diversified economic activities and incorporates other sectors into the "production chain," from the control of raw materials to the commercialization of commodities.

Financial capital's involvement in agriculture fuels speculation on farmland at the global level, but at the country level the process of territorialization and appropriation of land rent varies. Speculation on agricultural commodities in financial markets increases food prices, which has a disproportional impact on low-income households, which spend a larger percentage of their income on basic needs. In this context, peasant and

Indigenous communities have a key role, as they struggle to protect their land and food systems.

The Industrialization of Agriculture

The current stage of monopoly capitalism demonstrates the dynamics of contradiction and complementarity between agricultural and industrial capital or between rural and urban sectors. The process of capital expansion in the countryside favours industrial sectors, especially transnational corporations that benefit from a system based on chemical inputs. But monopoly control of agricultural production also reveals a dialectical relationship between economic crisis and capital accumulation. A series of crises in the sector reveal that agribusiness corporations benefit from state policies, subsidies and special lines of credit, most of which go to financing industrial inputs.

A historical analysis of these crises shows that they are not merely the result of conjunctural elements, such as fluctuations in commodity prices and an imbalance between supply and demand. Agribusiness representatives promote these justifications for their crises to demand financial support from governments and legitimize the intensive use of industrial inputs in agriculture. The industrialization of agriculture requires increasing amounts of constant capital. Large corporations usually do not take much risk when making these investments because they receive the highest percentage of state subsidies, such as credit offered at subsidized interest rates. Credit systems regulate the price of money as a commodity, so when interest rates are low or subsidized, the price of money is low. These resources, which corporations commonly call "investments," constitute a transfer of social surplus value to the private sector, which is usually mediated by the state.

When explaining capital-land-labour relations in the trinity formula, Marx challenged the fetishist perception through which the product of capital (including industrial and financial capital) appears as profits, the product of labour appears as wages and land appears as a source of income. Marx clarified that surplus value is the source of these three elements due to the particular form that abstract labour takes in capitalist social relations. The concept of fetishism is central in Marx's theory of value because it explains the dialectical relation between "essence" and "appearance" or concrete abstraction. Appearance is understood as an abstraction that is expressed or materialized in capitalist social relations mediated by the commodity form.

The development of productive forces in capitalist relations is motivated by the movement of capital reproduction in search of valorization and accumulation. Therefore, the production of commodities and technological innovations become consequences of this process. This movement generates contradictions within the organic composition of capital, such as a tendency for the profit rate to fall associated with an increase in labour productivity. In the agribusiness system, this process is characterized by a growing market concentration, especially in the production of industrial inputs and commercialization. Another key aspect is the speculative role of financial markets in agriculture, including futures commodity markets and farmland markets, as consequences of crises of overaccumulation.

Agribusiness corporations' speculation in financial markets reflects the simultaneous, dialectical relation between crisis and accumulation. In the case of futures commodity markets, the time of commercialization becomes fictional since these negotiations are based on future projections of production. In farmland markets, the main objective of financial and agribusiness corporations is to control land but not necessarily the production of agricultural commodities. However, to justify these deals and influence land prices so that they rise, these corporations promote the expansion of industrial monocrop plantations, which have destructive impacts on natural resources such as biodiversity and water sources. The result over time is a decrease in land prices and productivity as soil fertility deteriorates, leading to new cycles of territorial expansion and environmental destruction. Gaining control of natural resources and raw materials, incorporating agricultural production into industrial sectors, increasing labour exploitation and expanding international trade are strategies used by agribusiness corporations to deal with crises of overaccumulation.

These strategies are also associated with neocolonial or imperialist elements of capitalist reproduction. Luxemburg (1985) identified this as a specific method of accumulation, explaining imperialism as not only a phase of capitalism but also a permanent mechanism of capital accumulation. She also defined the dual role of militarism as an incentive to increase labour productivity in imperialist countries and to transfer social surplus value to the state and private corporations. States use these strategies to justify military interventions that expand foreign trade and the appropriation of raw materials in peripheral countries.

Luxemburg (1985: 364–92) observed critical aspects of capitalist reproduction as the appropriation of surplus value associated with a permanent imperialist strategy. She challenged the deterministic views of Karl Kautsky and Otto Bauer, who defended imperialist mechanisms, as they imagined that those geopolitical strategies would promote technical progress and industrialization internationally. Luxemburg opposed Kautsky's nationalist position in the beginning of the twentieth century, when he defended foreign interventions in the name of the imperialist nation-state.

The development of productive forces as a characteristic of the capitalist mode of production and its particular forms of capital-labour relations are expressed through competition, but competition is not only a result of technological innovation, since the creation of new technologies to increase labour productivity also occurred in precapitalist societies. Marx defined the singularity of capital-labour relations in capitalism using the concept of labour as a concrete abstraction, explaining that technological innovations are stimulated by competition or the possibility of exploiting surplus value. Competition is a determining factor in the development of productive forces and, simultaneously (dialectically), an element of rationality or coercion in a predominantly irrational movement of increasing monopoly capital, generated by competition while also eliminating competition. This type of capital concentration is typical of crises of overaccumulation.

Today, the deterministic notion of development is commonly used to characterize "developing countries." This definition creates the impression that these countries are on an ideal, linear path to economic development. Mônica Martins (2008: 23–24) criticized this view by explaining that "underdevelopment and development are not stages of growth; they stem from the worldwide expansion of capitalism and its imperialist logic. Therefore, this process is not based on resource allocation, but on the way in which capital exploits resources within national and regional spaces to increase accumulation."

The contradictory movement of crisis and accumulation also explains the tendency of imperialist countries to export capital in its financial and industrial forms to countries where the costs of labour and raw materials are lower. The beginning of this process was characterized by the concentration of financial capital in the hands of large banks that had a growing influence over industrial production. National states also favoured large corporations by granting them credit, which resulted in capital concentration in strategic economic sectors. The formation of a financial oligarchy consolidated the monopolization of certain economic sectors through trusts or cartels, eliminating capitalist competition.

The role of financial capital today shows that the availability of credit granted to corporations by states does not guarantee that these resources will be used as productive capital. The concentration of financial capital generates speculative tendencies, including in farmland markets. The global movement of financial capital produces abstract spaces that ignore national borders, such as in "free" trade agreements in which "free" only applies to capital, not to labour.

The deregulation of financial markets began in the 1950s with the economic hegemony of the United States and its "reconstruction" project in Europe. This postwar period generated capital accumulation from wages and pensions in the banking system. In addition to the banking sector, other institutions began to operate in interest-bearing capital markets, including pension funds and insurance companies. This movement represented a huge transfer of social surplus value to the private sector. François Chesnais (2005: 38) noted that the "influx of uninvested resources accelerated in the early 1970s, as the dynamism of the 'golden age' wore off. Governments were forced to extend its duration by increasing credit." One of the mechanisms created to guarantee the availability of credit was the possibility of trading state debt on financial markets.

The root of this process is in the particular form that private property takes as "patrimonial property" through the figure of the "owner-shareholder" or "rentier." The speculative nature of financial markets means that patrimonial property "is related to the fetishist character, perfectly mystifying 'values' supposedly created in financial markets" (Chesnais 2005: 58). Fetishism means the naturalization of the idea that financial capital can reproduce itself. The expectation of profitability in financial markets characterizes fictitious capital since it is not necessarily based on the production process. Fictitious capital appears to generate profits independently from the material basis of the production process, which gives it a fetishistic character. Marx (1985, vol. 3: 279) ironically compared this to the function of a "pear tree," which is "giving pears."

After World War II, the adoption of the US dollar as the main currency for international trade facilitated market concentration and the consolidation of transnational corporations, including in industrial agriculture. In the 1970s, this process of apparent expansion resulted in a global economic crisis. Capital in the form of money became increasingly detached from the production process, stimulating the export of financial capital in search of valorization to the periphery of the economic system. This was the cause of the debt crisis in Latin America in the 1980s, when the industrialization of agriculture increased in the region.

Between 1969 and 1976, the average annual increase in rural credit in Brazil was 23.8 percent (Delgado 1985: 46). The expansion of credit for agriculture is related to elements of instability and economic crisis. The credit crisis had impacts on industrial agricultural production and commercialization. In Brazil, state credit for commercialization, which included the guarantee of minimum prices, prioritized industrialized sectors. In the 1977–78 harvest, individual producers received 13.3 percent of state credit;

cooperatives, 21.9 percent; and agribusiness and trade corporation, 64.8 percent. In the 1978–79 harvest, individual producers received 4.8 percent; cooperatives, 22.5 percent; and agribusiness and trade corporations, 72.7 percent. Then, in the 1979–80 harvest, individual producers received 7.8 percent; cooperatives, 23 percent; and agribusiness and trade corporations, 69.2 percent (Delgado 1985: 87).

Some of the main effects of the economic crisis in peripheral countries were exchange rate fluctuations and increasing interest rates, which led to the debt crisis or the "lost decade" of the 1980s. Structural adjustment policies allegedly adopted to address this crisis worsened inequality in urban and rural areas. In Brazil, the debt service reached 96 percent of Brazilian export earnings by 1986 (Oliveira 1998: 302–303). At that time, giving priority to state support for mechanized agriculture was justified as necessary to pay off the external debt and improve the trade balance. But the country's dependency on industrial inputs for agriculture contributed to the trade deficit.

In the 1990s, neoliberal policies continued to be implemented and were expanded using the same argument (to deal with the debt crisis). The result was devastating, as transnational corporations took control over strategic economic sectors such as energy, agriculture, mining, telecommunications, water, sanitation, healthcare and education. The privatization of pension and retirement funds also caused greater financial instability, as did the payments of foreign debt services at floating interest rates. When financial capital determines the production process, a floating interest rate system stimulates financial speculation and benefits agroindustrial monopolies that have privileged access to credit at subsidized interest rates.

In agribusiness systems, a growing percentage of immobilized constant capital is formed by industrial inputs, and land as a productive base also constitutes a limit for the circulation of capital. However, since the 1980s, financial deregulation has generated new mechanisms such as financial derivatives that facilitate the circulation of capital based on multiple transactions using land as an asset. Moments of capital circulation in financial markets and moments of capital immobility in assets such as land and fixed capital are combined as corporations consolidate such assets to access more credit.

Land markets, characterized by financial transactions based on property titles, connect distinct operations of financial capital. Land markets and financial markets are intertwined in the movement of crisis and accumulation of capital. Increasing land prices due to speculation stimulates the circulation of capital in its financial or fictitious form. The expansion of land markets involves operations of banks, insurance, real estate and agribusiness corporations. States also have a role in this process, for example, in transferring public land to the private sector, in addition to providing subsidized credit and tax incentives to large corporations.

The Industrialization of Agriculture in Brazil

One theoretical perspective about the industrialization of agriculture in Brazil imagines that feudalism guaranteed the historical conditions necessary for the development of productive forces in capitalism. This interpretation of history sees peasants as "feudal remains" in today's society, and it is based on the assumption that feudal relations along European lines existed in other parts of the world. Prado Jr. (2007: 65) disputed this type of argument:

> It is very important to accurately characterize the true nature of labour relations in Brazilian agriculture … especially because in many cases, the formal aspect that they assume can lead to confusion that, in practice, prove to be highly inconvenient. This is how these relationships are often described as having a "feudal" or "semifeudal" nature. Strictly speaking, similar to any other term with an equally pejorative and emotional charge, the expression "feudal" could be used to designate certain extremely brutal forms of labour exploitation. It would be a simple matter of linguistic inconvenience, were it not for the connotations that the term has, and the inconveniences that derive from it, both theoretical and practical.[1]

Prado Jr.'s critique refers to the stage-based methodological view that ignores that the transition from feudalism to capitalism in the European context was based on violence as a "productive force" fuelled by colonial relations. The theoretical perspective that sees remnants of feudalism in Brazil influenced the debate about the industrialization of agriculture, especially after the 1960s.

In contrast with the Brazilian geopolitical context, the United States broke away from the colonial model established in England at the beginning of the industrialization period, which expanded the proletariat internally and demanded imports of raw materials from the colonies. The war for independence in the United States changed the international division of labour associated with colonialism (McMichael 2000).

The concept of agribusiness was disseminated in Brazil in connection with the system of production chains, which include industrial inputs (pesticides, fertilizers, genetically modified seeds and machinery), as well as wholesale and retail distribution, packaging, transportation, fuel, road concessionaires and port services. Marcos Sawaya Jank, one of the sector's ideologues, defined this concept in an article published by Brazilian newspaper *O Estado de São Paulo* on May 7, 2005:

> Agribusiness is nothing more than a conceptual framework that delimits integrated systems that produce food, fibres and biomass, whose operations range from genetic improvements to the final product, and in which all agents who aim to produce agricultural raw materials must inevitably become integrated, whether they are small or large producers, family or corporate farmers, large landowners or settlers.

The idea that all social segments of the Brazilian countryside should "inevitably become integrated" into agribusiness suggests a "natural" and irreversible process. This type of ideology reveals the context of social relations in which the concept of agribusiness is constructed and disseminated, ignoring the history of colonization and land concentration in the country.

Monopolies over land and agricultural policies that were designed to give priority to meeting the demands of foreign markets characterized the role of colonial Brazil as a "country-corporation" (Prado Jr. 1970) that exports agricultural and mineral commodities such as gold, sugar, tobacco, cotton and coffee. This economic system continues today, but even under this policy, small farmers produce most of the food for internal markets in the country. According to the 2006 agricultural census, smallholder agriculture produced 84 percent of yuca, 67 percent of beans, 52 percent of milk, 49 percent of corn, 40 percent of poultry and eggs and 31 percent of rice (Instituto Brasileiro de Geografia e Estatística 2006).

The "integration" of agriculture and industry was described by Alberto Passos Guimarães (2009) as the formation of the "agroindustrial complex." Guimarães identified that the agroindustrial complex concept was formulated in the United States and Europe in the 1950s and described its implementation in Brazil as a "conservative modernization" policy limited to the use of machinery, since it maintained the unequal structure of land ownership. The idea of "conservative modernization" in agriculture outlines a system that is dependent on industrial inputs and state subsidies, and that maintains land concentration and the power of rural oligarchies. This system is based on the "integration" and "subordination" of agriculture to industrial and financial corporations. Guimarães (1978) predicted that this process would generate a structural crisis in agriculture due to an increase in production costs and a decrease in the average profit rate.

A comparative analysis by the Brazilian Institute of Geography and Statistics on data from agricultural censuses carried out from 1940 to 1970 shows that production tripled in Brazil during this period. In these thirty years, the price of fertilizer increased twenty times; the cost of pesticides, eight times; the cost of seeds, seedlings and feed, thirty times, and machines and vehicles, four times. Production costs increased from 7.25 percent to 19.88 percent in relation to the price of agricultural production. In 1976, the industrial agriculture sector accumulated a debt of US$13 billion (Guimarães 1978: 131–33).

This increase in production costs coincided with a growing presence of foreign agribusiness corporations in Brazil, which monopolized the production of inputs and machinery, as well as commercialization. This resulted in a transfer of income from agriculture to industrial sectors. The largest multinational corporations operating in the Brazilian agroindustrial sector at that time were Ford Motors, Unilever, Hoechst, E.I. Du Pont de Nemours, Nestlé, British-American Tobacco, Phillips Petroleum, Fiat, General Foods, Borden, Ralston Purina, Continental Can, Coca-Cola, CPC International, Phillip Morris, Massey Ferguson, Gervais Danone, PepsiCo, Standard Brands, Central Soya, Quaker Oats, Del Monte, Kellogg's, Heublein and Anderson Clayton. Also, among the largest subsidiaries of foreign corporations in Brazil were the Rockefeller Group, Bunge, Cargill, BASF and Aracruz Celulose (Guimarães 1978: 135).

In the 1970s, Brazilian agriculture became a major market for international industrial inputs, which had a significant impact on the external debt. During that period, 50 percent of agricultural inputs in Brazil changed from a natural base to industrial products, and about half of agricultural production was done to satisfy foreign corporations' demand for raw materials (Müller 1989: 31–37). The expansion of agribusiness has also caused the displacement of rural communities and migration to urban areas, especially since the 1980s.

Dependency on machinery and chemical inputs generated a structural agrarian crisis characterized by higher demand for state subsidies and the indebtedness of the agroindustrial complex. Other consequences of this process were rising farmland prices, control of agricultural commodity prices by foreign corporations and the expansion of the "agricultural frontier," which caused environmental destruction, higher land concentration and less diversity in food production. Advertising campaigns by agribusiness corporations promoted the consumption of industrialized foods, changing eating habits in Brazil and internationally.

The expansion of the agroindustrial complex deepened Brazil's role as a supplier of agricultural raw materials based on external demand. This system generated a double dependency on access to credit to cover increasing production costs, which stemmed from the use of machinery and chemical inputs whose production was controlled by multinational corporations. State credit and subsidies for agribusiness represented a transfer of social surplus value to private agroindustrial monopolies and stimulated speculation on agricultural commodities in financial markets.

Archives of economic publications in Brazil illustrate this transformation in the agricultural system and the social, economic and political processes that popularized the concept of agribusiness. In the 1960s, coffee was the main export product in Brazil, but the country had a diversified list of commodities traded on international stock exchanges that also included meat, corn, sugar, soybeans, wheat, milk, oats, rice, beans, cotton, rye, cocoa, castor oil, rubber, cloves, cinnamon and leather. In addition to a greater degree of agriculture diversification, the state had more control over food stocks, export quotas and commercial policies for controlling agricultural imports and preventing dumping.

At that time, the debate about land concentration and the need for agrarian reform and regional integration trade agreements in Latin America permeated the political scenario. Agrarian reform was a main proposal of President João Goulart's administration. He was also engaged in the creation of the Latin American Free Trade Association (Associação Latino-Americana de Livre Comércio) to facilitate regional integration. Goulart's government suffered a military coup in 1964 and was not able to implement reforms to change the land structure in Brazil — a country where the level of land concentration is one of the highest in the world even today. During the military dictatorship, state support for food production for the domestic market was part of a policy that aimed to subsidize the reproduction of the workforce for industrial sectors that were being established in Brazil to keep wages low.

In the 1980s, the US government and corporations began to facilitate the expansion of soy production in Brazil as a noncompetitive foreign policy due to increasing demand from China and oil-exporting countries, such as Venezuela and ones in the Middle East. In turn, US corporations increased exports of industrial agricultural inputs to Brazil under the slogan of the "green revolution," which generated greater dependency on machinery and chemical inputs.

Internationally, the Cold War context was characterized by the intensification of capital exports from central countries to the periphery of capitalism, which generated the debt crisis in Latin America during the 1980s. This context also intensified tensions in international relations as several countries declared a moratorium on debt payments. The debt crisis in Latin America served as an excuse for governments to implement neoliberal policies, including structural adjustment measures, arguing that there was a need to establish a "minimal state." Neoliberal policies aggravated the debt crisis, mainly by deregulating interest rates and generating higher levels of economic inequality. These policies were promoted more aggressively internationally during the Ronald Reagan administration in the United States and the Margaret Thatcher administration in England. These countries disseminated a discourse in favour of commercial deregulation, condemning the "protectionism and interventionism" of the Brazilian state in agriculture.

The end of the military dictatorship in Brazil created important spaces for social and political organizing for agrarian reform and labour rights. However, neoliberal policies adopted since the 1980s promoted fiscal "austerity" and "free" trade as solutions to the external debt crisis. The negotiations of trade agreements such as the General Agreement on Tariffs and Trade were justified as a way to deal with the debt crisis. Arguments in defence of "free" trade and the privatization of public sectors used the idea that Brazil would be "rewarded" by foreign creditors. Policies included privatizing key economic sectors, increasing food imports and deregulating food stocks. At that time, Brazilian agricultural commodities traded on the stock exchange were reduced to mainly cocoa, orange juice, coffee, sugar and soy. The social demands for agrarian reform were not heeded and the rural exodus aggravated poverty in urban centres.

Neoliberal policies stimulated the concentration of private capital in agriculture through the "productive partnerships" or joint ventures between Brazilian rural oligarchies and foreign agribusiness corporations. Usually, these corporations received state subsidies from the National Bank for Economic and Social Development (BNDES). The promoters of agribusiness preached the downsizing of the state while also demanding governmental subsidies and promoting private monopolies as "strategic alliances." Private monopolies in agricultural production and marketing were also stimulated by the role of financial capital, which included strengthening futures markets and other financial mechanisms used by agribusiness corporations that had access to subsidized state credit. Speculation with agricultural commodities generated instability in food prices. This mechanism for inflating food prices was aggravated by trade deregulation, which also facilitated the dumping of food in Brazil and in other countries in the Global South.

Despite constant crises, agribusiness is frequently presented in a positive way and associated with "development" by mainstream media in Brazil. However, an economic analysis of different historical periods shows that state subsidies for agribusiness exceeded the country's trade surplus. In 1980, for example, the government cancelled US$13 billion of the agribusiness sector's debt, which was twice the announced trade surplus for the sector. Despite its access to various types of subsidies and tax incentives, agribusiness corporations maintained high debt levels. In 1999, the Brazilian government wrote off US$18 billion of the sector's debt; the announced trade surplus for that year was US$10 billion.

In addition to these constant debt rollovers, several trade policies were designed to consolidate commercial advantages for the agricultural sector based on monocropping for export. Foreign policy in favour of agribusiness included state lobbying to expand its market access and infrastructure. An example was the 1996 approval of the Kandir Law, which created new tax incentives for agricultural exports. During the 1990s, a period identified with the implementation of neoliberal policies and the defence of a "minimum" state, the Brazilian government continued to provide support for agribusiness under the claim that it would generate a trade balance.

The history of debt rollovers shows that the principal business of agribusiness is access to subsidized credit. Therefore, the main "product" of agribusiness is not, for example, soy, sugarcane, eucalyptus or meat (the main agricultural commodities produced in Brazil today), but debt itself. Agribusiness corporations seek to inflate their economic assets, such as land, machinery and stocks, to increase their bargaining power with governments so they maintain the subsidies, even if these corporations accumulate debt.

Land as a financial asset facilitates the circulation of capital based on multiple transactions on financial markets. In addition to the greater immobility of constant capital generated by agribusiness's dependency on industrial inputs, land as a productive base would theoretically represent a limit for the circulation of capital. However, it now functions as a financial asset through speculative mechanisms. The alternation between moments of circulation of financial capital and capital immobility expressed in fixed capital aims to present such assets as guarantees to access credit. The detachment of capital in the form of money from the productive process stimulated the industrialization of agriculture in Brazil, as well as territorial expansion of the so-called agricultural frontier, rural exodus to urban areas and market concentration. Monopoly over land also limited Brazil's autonomy in food production and the possibility of building food sovereignty.

Historically and currently, the agribusiness lobby has used its political power to continue receiving state subsidies to expand monocrop plantations, mainly in areas with access to infrastructure, vast water sources and biodiversity. The territorial expansion of agribusiness causes the destruction of natural resources and intensifies capital concentration. These processes of extensive territorial expansion and intensive capital concentration constitute a context of crisis and accumulation. Capital concentration in agribusiness also intensifies the "migration" of foreign financial capital to farmland markets, as a speculative movement that stimulates an increase in land prices and joint ventures between transnational corporations and the Brazilian rural oligarchy. The following chapters demonstrate how farmland in Brazil became a main target of financial speculation, especially after the global economic crisis and the collapse of the housing market in the United States in 2007–08.

Notes

1. Original in Portuguese: "É muito importante a caracterização precisa da verdadeira natureza das relações de trabalho na agropecuária brasileira ... sobretudo porque em muitos casos o aspecto formal de que se revestem leva ou pode levar a confusões que na prática se revelam da maior inconveniência. É assim a qualificação que frequentemente se faz dessas relações como sendo de natureza 'feudal' ou 'semifeudal.' Em rigor, a expressão 'feudal' poderia servir, como qualquer outra de igual carga pejorativa e emocional, para designar certas formas extremamente brutais de exploração do trabalho. Seria uma simples questão de inconveniência lingüística, não fossem as conotações que o termo comporta, e os inconvenientes que daí derivam, tanto de ordem teórica, como prática."

3 Socioeconomic Impacts of Financial Speculation and Land-Grabbing

The pandemic caused by Covid-19 and the current global environmental crisis demand a deep reflection on the use of land and the urgent need to protect biodiversity and support ecological agriculture that produces healthy and affordable food in local markets. A main cause of climate change is the expansion of industrial agriculture (UNCTAD 2013) based on the use of chemical inputs that destroy the soil and water sources. In Brazil, widespread fires in the Amazon (rainforest), Pantanal (wetlands) and Cerrado (savannah) biomes have been unprecedented in number and scale in recent years (Borges and Branford 2020).

Especially after the global financial crisis of 2008 and the collapse of the housing market in the United States, international agribusiness and financial corporations formed alliances with rural oligarchies to operate in Brazilian farmland markets. The economic crisis generated a change in the profile of agribusiness in Brazil through mergers and joint ventures not only with foreign agricultural corporations but also with financial groups and oil companies (Xavier, Pitta and Mendonça 2011). These mergers increased their assets, such as land, machinery and subsidiaries. As corporations concentrated their operations, the increase in the price of their shares in stock markets facilitated their access to credit in order to expand further.

Beginning in 2002, agribusiness corporations in Brazil took advantage of high commodity prices in international markets, which generated a greater level of indebtedness, as in the case of the sugarcane sector. These companies contracted debt in US dollars with the expectation of increasing future exports. The mills negotiated export contracts on futures markets, which influenced their territorial expansion and mechanization. This process stimulated inflation in the price of agricultural land. At the same time, promises of future production by companies that had previous debts fuelled new indebtedness and further territorial expansion. The strategy of financing existing debts with new funds based on futures markets led to a dialectical process of accumulation and crisis, which intensified labour exploitation and the predatory use of natural resources (Mendonça 2018).

As of 2008, when the price of sugar began to fall along with agricultural commodity prices in general, several Brazilian sugarcane companies went bankrupt (Mendonça, Pitta and Xavier 2012). However, the reduction of agricultural commodity prices did not affect the price of farmland in Brazil, which continued to rise and attract international financial corporations, such as the US-based pension fund Teachers Insurance and Annuity Association (TIAA) and the Harvard Management Company, which manages Harvard University's endowment fund (Friends of the Earth US, GRAIN, National Family Farm Coalition and Rede Social de Justiça e Direitos Humanos 2019). The social and environmental impacts of this business are felt today.

International Financial Corporations and Land Speculation in Brazil

The global economic crisis that became apparent in 2008 intensified the role of financial capital in farmland markets around the world. Land speculation facilitates the circulation of financial capital in a context of international economic instability. This trend is stimulated by foreign investment funds' search for new assets. After the economic crisis of 2008, the possibility of Brazilian agribusiness corporations accessing credit on the basis of promising future production declined significantly (Pitta 2016). With the sharp drop in agricultural commodity prices, many sugar and ethanol mills with debts in US dollars went bankrupt. This context led to mergers as a strategy for companies to increase their assets in order to access new credit.

One example was the creation of a rural real estate company, Radar Agricultural Properties, in 2008 as a joint venture between the largest sugarcane corporation in Brazil, Cosan, and a financial company, Mansilla. Originally, Cosan held 18.9 percent of Radar's shares, while Mansilla was the main shareholder at that time. Data from 2012 indicate that Radar controlled 151,468 hectares of land, estimated at R$2.35 billion, or about US$1 billion. That year, land prices rose by an average of 56 percent, and Radar's portfolio increased 93 percent compared to 2011. Radar owns at least 555 properties in Brazil, which together add up to approximately 270,000 hectares of land, with a declared value of R$5.2 billion (Mendonça, Pitta and Xavier 2014).

The principal source of capital for Radar's operations in Brazil came from TIAA, which manages pension funds in the United States valued at approximately US$1 trillion. To operate in international land markets, TIAA created a subsidiary, TIAA-CREF Global Agriculture LLC, which is now called Nuveen. It also collected interest-bearing capital from other sources such as the AP2 pension fund from Sweden; Caisse de Dépôts et Placement du Québec; the British Columbia Investment Management Corporation; Stichting Pensioenfonds ABP from the Netherlands; Ärzteversorgung Westfalen-Lippe from Germany; Cummins UK Pension Plan Trustee, the Environment Agency Pension Fund and the Greater Manchester Pension Fund from England; and the New Mexico State Investment Council in the United States (Pitta, Cerdas and Mendonça 2018).

When a large corporation such as TIAA creates specific funds to operate in farmland markets, the result is a speculative process that inflates land prices, even if the prices of agricultural commodities decrease. This reveals a disconnection between land markets and commodity markets, which explains the speculative nature of these tendencies. To justify the increase in land prices, these companies stimulate the expansion of monocropping of agricultural commodities such as sugarcane, soybean, genetically modified corn, cotton and eucalyptus, with devastating environmental and social impacts.

Harvard University also plays a key role in promoting speculation on farmland. In the first decade after the 2008 economic crisis, Harvard Management Company acquired over 850,000 hectares of farmland globally by channelling about US$930 million to its subsidiaries. Some of these companies were registered in tax havens, as part of a strategy to hide the nature and scope of this business. By 2016, Harvard subsidiaries controlled over forty farms in Brazil on approximately 405,000 hectares of land (GRAIN and Rede Social de Justiça e Direitos Humanos 2018).

Other agricultural real estate companies have been created in recent years. SLC Agricola (Schneider Logemann Company Agricola), for example, which is the largest grain producer in Brazil, manages SLC Land in partnership with international pension funds. Speculation in the Brazilian farmland market combines the operations of pension funds and real estate, agribusiness and financial corporations. The state also plays a central role by financing and handing over public land to the private sector. Even if financial corporations do not acquire farmland directly, they stimulate speculation on the price of farmland by funding Brazilian subsidiaries, which generates vulnerability for small farmers, Indigenous Peoples and other rural communities.

To start operating in Brazil, TIAA used subsidiary companies such as Mansilla, Tellus and Nova Gaia Brasil Participações to channel foreign capital into farmland markets because of a Brazilian law that limits ownership of land by foreigners. This process allowed, for example, Tellus to float debentures (a fixed-rate debt instrument) on financial markets, which were bought by Radar and Nova Gaia. The initial investment came from Cosan and TIAA, although it appeared to come from several sources. Tellus then used these resources to buy farmland through other subsidiaries or "financial vehicles" (Pitta, Cerdas and Mendonça 2018).

This process reveals how international pension funds promote a type of "outsourcing" of land deals that uses local companies to operate in Brazil as a way to avoid responsibility for violating land ownership laws while causing the displacement of rural communities and environmental destruction. The outsourcing mechanism consists of creating several companies with the same administrators, as well as subsidiaries, to make it appear as though they belong to different owners. These companies then negotiate land among themselves. For example, Cosan and TIAA (through other companies such as Mansilla and TerraViva Brasil Participações Ltda) are partners in Radar and Tellus.

Outsourcing land deals is one strategy that international pension funds use to insulate themselves from liability for the harmful impacts of land speculation, as they consider themselves "partners" in these deals. Further, the creation of several interrelated companies serves to obscure the location of the farms they are dealing with. The outsourcing strategy among these companies shields investors from being considered direct landowners, thus exempting them from responsibility for the social and environmental impacts of this business.

TIAA and Harvard University are the largest foreign buyers of farmland in Brazil, and they both channel foreign funds to Brazilian subsidiaries to circumvent a Brazilian law that limits foreign ownership of land. Since 2008, they have amassed a combined total of around 750,000 hectares of farmland in Brazil, mostly in the northeastern part of the Cerrado biome. These companies use opaque corporate structures, including offshore jurisdictions, to conceal their ownership and evade Brazilian legislation. But in 2020, an investigation by the Public Prosecutor's Office and the National Institute for Agrarian Reform (INCRA) in Brazil exposed how Harvard University and TIAA circumvented Brazilian laws to acquire farms in regions where local communities had been displaced. INCRA's report on the purchase of land by TIAA after 2010 showed how the pension fund violated Brazilian laws governing the acquisition of farmlands by foreign entities. In INCRA's view, TIAA's land purchases were carried out via the company Radar Propriedades Agrícolas and other Brazilian subsidiaries, which should be considered part of the same economic group. As a result, INCRA recommended that all the land purchases carried out via TIAA's subsidiaries since 2010 (more than 150,000 hectares) be annulled and voided (Associação de Advogados de Trabalhadores Rurais, GRAIN and Rede Social de Justiça e Direitos Humanos 2020).

Similar to TIAA, Harvard University uses subsidiaries, such as Terracal, Caracol Agropecuária and Insolo Agroindustrial, to operate in Brazil's farmland markets (GRAIN and Rede Social de Justiça e Direitos Humanos 2018). In October 2020, the court in the Brazilian state of Bahia issued a sentence blocking the registration of lands for one of Harvard's largest farmland acquisitions in Brazil: an agglomeration of 107,000 hectares of land known as the Gleba Campo Largo. The court also reopened an investigation into Harvard's acquisition of the Gleba Campo Largo based on evidence provided by the state prosecutor showing that this area was public land that had been illegally transferred to private owners. To avoid the consequences of these legal cases, Harvard's endowment fund has decided to spin off its farmland division into an independent private equity corporation called Solum Partners, which has the AIG insurance group as a partner (McDonald 2020). However, as INCRA's report on the TIAA case explained, under Brazilian law, foreign corporations and their subsidiaries should be considered part of the same economic group.

Local communities in Brazil are organizing to guarantee their land rights, demanding that Harvard University, TIAA and other financial corporations give their land back and pay reparations for social and environmental damages. They are building an international coalition called Stop Land Grabs in solidarity with faculty, staff and students at Harvard (Chaidez and Venkataramanan 2019) and other universities in the United States. As University of Iowa professors Laura R. Graham and Meena Khandelwal (2021) described,

> TIAA presents itself as a socially responsible investor; but TIAA's increasing farmland acquisitions are contributing to land-grabbing, deforestation and human rights violations. While claiming to ensure the future financial security for millions of U.S. middle-class workers, TIAA's investments are destroying the future for many rural communities and threatening the world's future through unsustainable agriculture.

Speculation on farmland has global consequences because the expansion of monocrop plantations is a main cause of climate change (Chaidez 2019).

Land-Grabbing in the Cerrado

Brazil's Cerrado is the most biodiverse savannah in the world, occupying an area of approximately 2.036 million square kilometres or 24 percent of the national territory. This biome contains 5 percent of the planet's biodiversity and Brazil's most important water basins. Its trees have very long roots that help replenish important sources of underground water, such as the Guarani, Bambuí and Urucuia aquifers, which contribute to the formation of two-thirds of Brazil's hydrographic regions, including the Amazon, Araguaia-Tocantins, Western Atlantic and Northeastern Atlantic, São Francisco, East Atlantic, Paraná and Paraguay (Ministério do Meio Ambiente 2006). Because of the Cerrado's location in the central plateaus of the country, vegetation is fundamental for maintaining the rain cycles needed for the preservation of other biomes, especially the Amazon but also the Pantanal (wetlands) and the Atlantic rainforest. The Cerrado is home to over eighty Indigenous ethnic groups, including the Karajá, AváCanoeiro, Krahô, Xavante, Xerente, Xacriabá and Tapuia (Barbosa 2008), and to a diversity of rural communities that use the land collectively and share the resources. The practices and knowledge of these communities are fundamental to environmental preservation.

The Matopiba region in the Cerrado — composed of the states of Maranhão, Tocantins, Piauí and Bahia — has been a prime target for farmland speculation by financial corporations that facilitate the expansion of monocrop plantations, especially soybeans and sugarcane. Agribusiness corporations also benefit from state-sponsored infrastructure projects, including roadways and railroads that connect the region to the commodity export terminals on the northeast coast, such as the ports of Itaqui in the state of Maranhão, Pecém in Ceará and Suape in Pernambuco.

This is the main region for the operations of TIAA, Harvard University and other financial corporations that negotiate land at low prices in the process of establishing farms. To introduce monocropping of commodities in these areas, agribusiness corporations destroy the native Cerrado vegetation and its rich biodiversity. Many farms are located in the *chapadas* (high plains) of the Cerrado and were established on public land through the displacement of peasant, Indigenous and Quilombola (rural Afro-Brazilian) communities that have lived in the region for many generations and whose right to the land is recognized by Brazilian law. The most common way to establish these farms is through land-grabbing, which consists of illegally forging land titles, fencing off areas, evicting local communities and then selling or leasing the "new" properties as if they were legalized. This illegal practice is known in Brazil as *grilagem*, which means storing counterfeit documents in boxes with crickets (*grilos* in Portuguese). The insects eat the paper, making the falsified documents look old so that they appear to be legitimate.

The expansion of monocropping and speculation with farmland in the high plains also affect the areas known as *baixões*, or lowlands, where rural communities have their houses and food production. Generally, agribusiness corporations expand monocropping of commodities in the *chapadas* using mechanized and irrigated agricultural systems, but they also expropriate the lowlands illegally as part of schemes that enable the "new landowners" to comply with regulations that require them to preserve forest cover on a certain percentage of their land (Pitta, Cerdas and Mendonça 2018). As a consequence, they destroy the biodiversity in the *chapadas* and enclose the lowlands. Many lowland areas have been illegally grabbed, causing the displacement of local communities. "We used to live off of fishing and farming. I can still remember the smell of rice when it was being harvested. But now, we can no longer grow our crops,"[1] explained a resident of a Quilombola community in the northeastern state of Piauí.

Another impact is the pollution of water sources. Agribusiness use of chemical inputs contaminates the river springs in the *chapadas*, which flow through the *baixões*. One of the main problems is the heavy use of pesticides that are sprayed by tractors and airplanes, affecting people's health and polluting their water and food production. A community member in the region described the issue:

> The water from the highlands flows down and fills our streams with agrochemicals. The water becomes muddy, and it stinks. In the river, we see fish floating on top of the water, dead. I didn't see the dead fish before. When we go fishing now, if we go in the morning, it takes us until noon to catch fish. There are no more fish in the river because of the poison."

Many times, communities have no alternative but to use contaminated water to bathe, cook and raise crops. "We sense the smell of a squashed tick. That's what I smell when I raise the glass to my mouth to drink. We sense that smell, but often we don't have any other water to drink."

A community resident in southern Piauí explained that soy plantations use at least three types of poison: "They do aerial spraying. Then, they use pesticides for worms directly on the ground and when the soybeans are already planted and ready to be harvested, they use a desiccant. And there is one more that they spray by plane, which gives us unbearable headaches." Chemical inputs used by agribusiness pollute the food production of communities in the *baixões*: "When the plane turns around, the poison falls on our production and burns our corn, beans, rice and broad beans."

Local residents have reported an increase in health concerns related to chemical inputs used in soy plantations: "I had never heard of cancer around here, but now there are many cases. Also, people are having vomiting attacks and diarrhea, like one little baby who has been very sick, vomiting and crying." Another problem is the "open-pit dump" that agribusiness corporations use to discard toxic materials such as pesticide packaging, as explained by a resident: "They made a dump on the mountain, and this is another way pesticides pollute our wetlands. The animals consume the garbage and die because everything is poisoned. They also drink the water and stay skinny, poisoned. It's not because of hunger, because here, everything is green. It's the toxic water that is killing our animals."

Many rivers have dried up in the Cerrado, as their water sources have been affected by deforestation as a result of the expansion of soybean plantations. Deforestation and pollution of river springs affect rainfall patterns in the whole region, cause the extinction of endangered species and destroy biodiversity. Agribusiness corporations benefit from fires in the region, as a resident of the local communities described: "We are very concerned with the fires because the fire destroys all the flora. The *pequi* flower burns, the cashew burns. It burns trees that provide food. The fires also cause damage to streams. Our streams are no longer filling."

Another cause of the fires is the flammability of pesticides used by agribusiness, as a community resident in Piauí explained: "Pesticides dry everything, toast everything, and are very dangerous because they stay in the soil and also increase the fires, reaching our areas." Community members also reported that setting fires was a strategy used by land grabbers: "They burn everything so that they can later pass the chains [used to uproot trees] to destroy the Cerrado vegetation and replace it with pasture or soy. Fire destroys the soil, and everything dies."

Violence against rural communities in the Cerrado and the Amazon frequently involves control over land, water and mining resources. As these biomes are interconnected, their devastation causes extreme climate crises in the whole hemisphere. As one community member stated, "Agribusiness plantations are a threat to our lives because deforestation is changing the climate, the rain, affecting our drinking water, our rivers and our food. The use of poison in their plantations brings plagues to our food production, like the white fly that destroys our harvest."

Rural communities, which have been struggling to secure land rights where they have lived for many generations, are threatened with violence to leave their homes. "We are afraid because we can be killed. One time, we were right here by our house when a car passed full of men armed with guns. They stopped and got out to mark spots on the ground where we live," explained a community resident.

Indigenous, Quilombola and peasant communities in the Cerrado are organizing against repression and calling for international solidarity to guarantee their collective land rights. As a result, the Gamela Indigenous community was able to wage a legal fight against a violent eviction on January 2021 and reclaim their territory of Morro D'Água in southern Piauí. A member of this Indigenous community described the violent displacement: "The gunmen arrived around 5 p.m. and set our house on fire, destroying almost everything inside. Also, we were not able to secure the food we planted, like our beans, corn, rice. We had to leave, but we exposed the violence and were able to return to our land."

The Morro D'Água community is demanding compensation for material and moral damages resulting from this illegal eviction by private gunmen, which happened during the Covid-19 pandemic (Rede Social de Justiça e Direitos Humanos 2021b). An Indigenous leader in Piauí talked about this organizing process:

> Many Indigenous Peoples are resisting the violence of the colonizers, land grabbers and businessmen who want to destroy the forest. Here, in Piauí, there are many Indigenous Peoples and we are organizing together: the Tabajara, Tapuio, Gamela and Cariri people. And we, as Indigenous women, are on the front line of this resistance to protect our food, our health, our water, our culture and our language. My community elected me to be a leader, which is not very common for a woman, but I feel strong and supported also by the young people in my community. I do everything I can to defend our territory because it is much more than our home; it represents our lives and the lives of our future generations.

Several rural communities in the region have formed a collective, with each sending representatives to meet on a regular basis to exchange knowledge and build strategies to protect their territories. An inspiring example is the *brejeira* (riverside) community of Salto, in the state of Piauí, which obtained its collective land title in June 2021 (Rede Social de Justiça e Direitos Humanos 2021a). As one resident explained, "We were able to guarantee our collective land rights and now, we are helping other communities to do the same. Now, we are more protected against land grabbers, and we hope that they will not come back again to burn our houses and displace us."

For rural communities, the granting of collective domain is an important step to protect their land rights, livelihoods, ecological food production and river springs. Agribusiness corporations use massive irrigation systems and pollute rivers in the Cerrado, but when local communities organize collectively, they are able to implement a strategy for recovering river springs in their territories. A local educator in a rural community reflected on this experience:

> When this idea started, I asked myself, "How can we recover our river springs?" It's difficult to imagine in theory, but in practice, it has been a wonderful experience that is happening in several communities. We planted trees close to the springs and protected the area. We exposed the fires and the poison from soy plantations of agribusiness. Little by little, we recovered the water, our source of life. Now, we have this knowledge that we can share with other people.

This organizing process allows communities to preserve their territories as a whole, instead of dividing the land into individual plots, so they maintain collective ways to produce food, raise animals, gather fruits and grow medicinal plants, preserving the Cerrado. "I have learned a lot with my parents and my grandparents about medicinal plants. We use them for many things, like the flu, pain, stomach problems. In our territory, we protect the Cerrado, which is very important for our culture and for our medicine," said a local resident.

The regularization of the land as collective property also protects the communities against financial speculation and land-grabbing, as small individual farmers are more vulnerable to these mechanisms. A member of the Salto community explained, "I'm thirty-five years old and during the collective organizing process, I realized that I was at least the seventh generation living here, and we learned about our family history." She also described how this process created closer relationships among community members: "We cultivate our food together and also help other communities plant corn, rice, beans, yuca, potato and raise our animals, like pigs, sheep and chicken."

Brazil has one of the highest levels of land concentration and income inequality in the world. Organizing for land rights is a key element to building social, economic and environmental justice. The displacement of rural communities forces them into degrading work on agribusiness plantations, often in slavery-like conditions. As work on most soy plantations is mechanized, the few jobs available are usually doing tasks such as spraying weeds, removing stones and stumps and clearing the land manually before seeding.

Agribusiness plantations usually try to entice youth in rural communities to do this type of work. One young person described what this is like:

> They promise a certain amount of money and working conditions, but after we start, they increase the work and pay much less. Now, I participate in a youth group because we are more vulnerable to exploitation when we are looking for a job. We raise awareness about forced labour on the plantations, including degrading working conditions and exhausting hours. When we don't accept these conditions, we may even face death threats. So I decided to come back to my community, organize young people and study agroecology because it's the best way to help my community.

Another community member spoke about food production and how they practice agroecology:

> When we eat the food we cultivate, we know that it's healthy because we don't use any pesticide. We know where our food comes from and so we know we are safe. We only use natural fertilizer on the land. We also preserve the forest and plant fruit trees together with the food we cultivate. One important element is to select and save our seeds to plant again next year. We do this together in the community and we also work together in the harvest. After the harvest we celebrate together.

Land concentration leads to further social and economic inequality, as rural communities are displaced from their lands and means of subsistence. When rural residents are forced to migrate to urban areas, their access to food and housing also deteriorates. A resident of the Salto community explained why she would never want to move to the city: "It is very peaceful here. We only hear the sounds of birds, of donkeys. The air is clean, and we can go fishing at night. We have a lot of fruit trees. You don't have anything like this in the city."

Financial Capital and Land Markets

Financial mechanisms that allow agribusiness corporations to present land as collateral in exchange for access to credit alternate between times when capital circulates more freely in financial markets and moments when the immobility of capital increases due to the need to invest in industrial supplies, such as chemical fertilizers, pesticides and machinery (Mendonça 2018). Speculation on land prices facilitates the circulation of financial capital, as agribusiness corporations operate in partnership with banking, insurance, real estate and industrial firms that are also involved in the expansion of land markets.

In the agribusiness system, in addition to constant capital's greater immobility due to dependency on industrial supplies, land as a productive base constitutes a limitation on the circulation of capital. This dependency explains the relation between financial markets and land markets, stimulating speculation on the price of commodities and land, as they function as a material basis for increasing the circulation of capital. The land market, characterized by financial operations involving land titles, plays the role of "unthawing and financing fixed capital investments" (Delgado 2012: 194). In this sense, land ownership is used as an asset to guarantee various transactions on financial markets.

Land markets and financial markets are intertwined in periods of economic crisis, as they stimulate capital accumulation. The industrialization of agriculture demands increasing amounts of credit, which largely benefit agribusiness corporations. In this production "chain," large multinational corporations control all sectors of the production and trading process. Market monopoly and capital concentration in agriculture lead to a crisis of overaccumulation, or the imbalance between constant and variable capital.

The industrialization of agriculture falls within the scope of the contradictory relation between economic crises and capital accumulation. Increasing costs of industrial inputs have fuelled the territorial expansion of agribusiness corporations and stimulated speculation on farmland prices. The state acts as a mediator, as public banks provide loans for agribusiness at subsidized interest rates. The international economic crisis that emerged in 2008 reaffirmed this trend, as financial capital's increased mobility was a determining factor that generated new cycles of debt for agribusiness corporations.

The development of productive forces in agriculture replaces labour with machinery. It does not, however, diminish the importance of centring an analysis on the capital-labour relation, even if labour is represented dialectically by its negative identity — that is, by the absence of labour. Competition between corporations functions as a determining factor in the development of productive forces and, simultaneously (dialectically), as an element of "rationality" or "coercion" in a predominately "irrational" move towards a greater concentration of capital and market monopoly. As a key factor in the capitalist mode of production, competition promotes higher levels of industrialization, which eliminates competition by excluding less productive companies from the market.

This process can be characterized as part of a crisis of overaccumulation, which is related to increasing deregulation of financial and land markets internationally. The role of pension funds in land market speculation generated a particular form or "appearance" that private property acquired in financial markets, described as "patrimonial property" — that is, through the figure of the "owner-shareholder" or "landlord" (Chesnais 2005: 48). This financial mechanism explains the role of fictitious capital, which "appears" as a source of profit even if it is disconnected from the production of commodities. The "appearance" of money generating value outside the production process constitutes its fetishist character. In other words, fetishism is the "naturalization" of the illusion that money is self-expanding in value.

While analyzing the role of financial capital, Chesnais (2005) looked back at policies introduced in the 1950s to deregulate the international credit system. The economic hegemony of the United States and the project to "rebuild" Europe during the post–World War II period led capital derived from the savings, salaries and retirement plans of workers to accumulate in the banking system. In addition to the concentration of financial capital by multinational banks, other institutions such as pension funds and insurance companies began to engage in operations involving interest-bearing capital. This process resulted in the transfer of an enormous amount of social surplus value to the private sector.

The industrialization of agriculture in Brazil and internationally replaced the technical basis of peasant farming with industrial supplies. To support this transition, the Brazilian government adopted a policy based on subsidized credit systems for agribusinesses and incentives for international commodity trade, which included tax incentives and new sources of funding for infrastructure. The creation of the National Rural Credit System (Sistema Nacional de Crédito Rural), which provided subsidized funding through state banks, in 1965 was essential for the promotion of the industrialization of agriculture. Between 1969 and 1976, rural credit increased on average 23.8 percent per year (Delgado 2012: 46). At the same time, fluctuations in financial markets and agricultural commodity markets generated economic instability and contributed to the external debt crisis in the 1980s. As agricultural commodities were turned into financial assets, speculation played a determining role in international market prices.

After the crisis of overaccumulation that marked the 1970s, new instruments to deregulate the international financial system emerged to facilitate the increase in capital flows towards peripheral countries, which led to the debt crisis in the 1980s. The continuity of credit systems in the 1990s was guaranteed through the creation of new financial mechanisms that allowed national states to renegotiate their foreign debts. In the following years, neoliberal policies were adopted as ways of creating financial tools to generate capital accumulation. The privatization of sectors that provided basic consumer goods and services with high profit potential, including energy, agriculture, mining, telecommunications, water, sanitation, health and education, benefited transnational corporations. Furthermore, the privatization of pension and retirement funds, together with the establishment of external debt payments at floating interest rates, increased financial accumulation.

During the period marked by neoliberal policies (1990–2002), regulations on foreign investors' profit remittances were relaxed. This process began with the deregulation of financial markets nationally and internationally. It also facilitated financial investments in government bonds and the transfer of revenues out of Brazil. This procedure is known as the "securitization of debt" (Belluzzo 2012) and allows various shareholders to trade the same financial asset. Among these assets are debts and shares of sugarcane and ethanol plants, as well as Brazilian government bonds traded on secondary markets. Brazil's capacity to roll over its internal debt (which exceeded its external debt in the 2000s) led the BNDES to offer new lines of subsidized credit for agribusiness, especially after the increase in agricultural commodities prices in 2003, which stimulated trading on the futures market. The international cycle of growth in commodity prices gained momentum after the crash of share prices on the Nasdaq Stock Exchange in 2001, which was stimulated by the burst of the dotcom bubble (Delgado 2012).

In addition, exporting capital by opening subsidiary companies in peripheral countries was a strategy used by multinational corporations to access cheaper labour and credit and tax benefits as well as appropriate raw materials and natural resources. Multinational corporations also benefited from trade and investment liberalization policies adopted in the 1990s. This international trend of greater capital mobility by multinational corporations is part of the logic of capital accumulation, but also reveals a contradictory process that combines "falling profit rates with phases of rapid financial accumulation" (Chesnais 2005: 60).

In the early 2000s, the upsurge in commodity prices allowed sugarcane plants in Brazil to take on higher levels of debt. These companies acquired debt in US dollars with trading corporations as they expected to earn returns from trading sugar as a commodity on the New York Stock Exchange and the futures market. Sugarcane corporations in Brazil traded future production to justify their territorial expansion and mechanization, which stimulated an increase in land prices. The strategy of financing existing debts with new funds based on futures markets led to a dialectical process of accumulation and crisis, which intensified labour exploitation and the use of natural resources.

Since 2008, international pension funds have become a key source of capital for agribusiness in Brazil, which allowed these companies to expand production through new debt rollovers. The sugarcane industry was affected by the eruption of the global financial crisis in 2008, as restrictions on access to credit forced several plants into bankruptcy. The crisis exposed agribusiness's dependency on debt rollovers to maintain productivity levels, as sugarcane companies increased their offer of shares on international markets, which served to inflate their assets to guarantee their access to credit. Even after the economic crisis, the sugarcane industry continued its territorial expansion. Despite the decline in productivity of sugarcane plantations since 2010, the concentration of land ownership has increased (Mendonça, Pitta and Xavier 2012).

The territorial expansion and production of sugarcane together increased in Brazil from 2004 to 2010. This changed with the 2011–12 harvest, when only territorial expansion increased. Analysis of the production area in comparison to the amount of sugarcane production per year indicates the average annual productivity during that period. In the 2004–05 harvest, sugarcane production yielded 73.89 tonnes per hectare. Productivity increased in the following years and reached 81.58 tonnes of sugarcane per hectare in the 2009–10 harvest. After that, it started to decrease, with an average of 77.44 tonnes per hectare in 2010–11 and 68.28 tonnes per hectare in 2011–12. During this period, only the larger sugarcane companies accessed new sources of credit, while several ethanol plants went into bankruptcy due to their growing debt, which currently exceeds the sector's revenues (Pitta 2011). In this context, land ownership is used as a means to access new credit lines.

The flow of financial capital into farmland markets fuelled speculation, causing sharp escalations in land and food prices. Even so, agricultural policies in Brazil continued to prioritize the provision of state support and subsidized credit to agribusiness corporations in much larger amounts than those available to small farmers who produce the majority of food for local consumption. According to the 2006 agricultural census, which was the latest to record this type of detailed information, small farmers produce 87 percent of cassava, 70 percent of beans, 46 percent of maize, 38 percent of coffee, 34 percent of rice, 58 percent of milk, 59 percent of swine, 50 percent of poultry, 30 percent of cattle and 21 percent of wheat (França, Grossi and Marques 2009).

In 2017, although the agricultural census did not register small farmers' production of specific products, it did indicate the level of land concentration in Brazil: 77 percent of all farm establishments were small farms, employing 67 percent of rural workers on only 23 percent of farmland (Ministério da Agricultura, Pecuária e Abastecimento 2020).

Even during periods of decreasing prices of agricultural commodities, agribusiness corporations received the large majority of governmental loans at subsidized interest rates. For the 2014–15 harvest period, they received R$156.1 billion, whereas the amount available for small farmers was R$24.1 billion. For the 2021–22 harvest period, the Brazilian government announced its subsidized credit plan, Plano Safra, in which R$39.34 billion (equivalent to about US$8 billion) were allocated to small farmers from a total of R$251.22 billion, even though the latest agricultural census indicated that small farmers constituted 77 percent of all farmers in Brazil (Ministério da Agricultura, Pecuária e Abastecimento 2021). These policies intensify the social impacts of financial intermediation and the industrialization of agriculture, as they stimulate further concentration of farmland for the production of a few commodities for export, such as soy, beef, timber and sugarcane, which replace food production for internal markets.

The territorial expansion of agribusiness in Brazil occurs mainly in regions that are rich in water sources, biodiversity and infrastructure. Agribusiness corporations increase their control of natural resources to generate returns on capital that has been immobilized in the form of investments in mechanization and chemical inputs. The social and environmental impacts of expanding monocropping of agricultural commodities affect food production by small farmers for local markets. Increases in food prices are also related to speculation in commodity markets, since agribusiness corporations use special governmental loans at subsidized interest rates to speculate on financial markets.

The sugar-energy industry justifies the territorial expansion of monocropping by alluding to the possibility of growth in the global demand for ethanol. After the international economic crisis in 2008, however, forecasts for this demand have changed. The instability of financial and commodity markets does not allow ethanol to provide energy security in Brazil or abroad. Its economic viability on a large scale depends on market conditions of two major international commodities — sugar and oil — meaning that ethanol functions not as a "leading" but a "supporting" actor in this context. Ethanol production is only commercially viable if the price of sugar is low (otherwise, most companies will choose to produce larger amounts of sugar instead of ethanol) and the price of oil is higher on the market. Consumers will not choose ethanol at the tanks if its cost is any higher than 70 percent of the price of gasoline because of the difference between the fuels in terms of performance. This explains why ethanol's commercial viability depends on sugar and oil.

Government discourse in support of agribusiness defends the goals of promoting a positive balance of trade, attracting foreign investments and increasing financial assets. While agricultural commodity prices were on the rise from 2003 until 2008, financial assets were also increasing, which made financial capital's intermediation appear as though it was generating profit from production. In the recessive phase after the 2008 crisis, asset prices and commodity prices started to deflate (Delgado 2012).

Despite constant crises, agribusiness corporations present themselves as promoters of economic "development" and overestimate their role in the Brazilian GDP, claiming to contribute between 30 and 40 percent when they only account for about 5 percent (Junior, Antonio and Goldfarb 2021). Agribusiness corporations inflate their supposed contribution to GDP by adding industrial and distribution sectors to this calculation. This positive image facilitates the agribusiness lobby's efforts to continue receiving state subsidies, to expand monocrop plantations and to appropriate natural resources. Monopolization of land hinders diversification of economic activities and allows agribusiness corporations to incorporate other sectors — from raw materials to the commercialization of commodities — into the so-called production chain.

The search for competitiveness on the world market has led the sugarcane industry, as well as other agribusiness corporations in Brazil, to acquire growing amounts of debt to maintain productivity at acceptable levels. In capitalism's current phase, corporations rely on financial interventions to inflate their assets. This process intensifies economic vulnerability as well as speculation on food and land markets. In a context where financial capital shapes economic policies, the adoption of a floating interest rate system constitutes a key factor for capital accumulation. Financial speculation stimulates an increase in agroindustrial monopolies with privileged access to state credit and subsidized interest rates.

This type of governmental credit system, commonly considered an "investment" that is supposed to represent a certain risk for corporations, actually constitutes a transfer of public funds to the private sector. The formation of monopolies ensures that major corporations are able to access special lines of credit and subsidies from governmental and private sources. Capital concentration in agribusiness intensifies the "migration" of foreign financial capital to target farmland in Brazil. The international credit system fuels financial markets and the "detachment" of capital in the form of money from the productive process, which stimulates the exportation of capital to the Global South in search of valorization. States play a key role in this process by transferring public land to the private sector, in addition to providing subsidized credit and tax incentives for large corporations.

As such, one may conclude that the main "product" of agribusiness is not, for instance, sugarcane, soybean, cattle or timber. Instead, it is the appropriation of capital either in its financial form through credit systems or through territorial expansion and the appropriation of natural resources such as land, water and biodiversity (Mendonça 2018). The search for valorization determines the role of foreign corporations in agriculture, which drives the expansion of monocrop plantations along the Brazilian agricultural "frontier" and increases in land prices, causing environmental destruction and the displacement of rural communities.

Another key element of analysis in the current economic and geopolitical disputes over land and natural resources is the connection between agriculture and energy markets. Agribusiness and oil corporations have used a discourse in defence of "green" energy to justify their increasing control over land to produce agrofuels. This process also stimulates financial speculation in farmland, as the following chapter illustrates.

Note

1. Interviews with rural community members were recorded in July 2020 in the states of Piauí and Bahia. For the safety of the interviewees, their names have not been disclosed. Original interviews in Portuguese were published in Stefano, Lima and Mendonça (2020). They were also included in the podcast series *Aqui é o meu lugar* (Rede Social de Justiça e Direitos Humanos 2020).

4 The Myth of Agrofuels

The need to increase support for renewable energy sources is central to dealing with the global climate crisis. Brazil's impact on climate change is largely a consequence of environmental destruction by the expansion of agribusiness in the Cerrado (*Guardian* 2022), the Pantanal (Pesquisa Fapesp n.d.) and the Amazon (Bowman 2021). Expanding plantations to produce agrofuels[1] accelerates deforestation and, therefore, the concept of renewable energy should be discussed from a broader perspective that considers the impacts of the whole production process. In Brazil, the ethanol produced from sugarcane has been presented as "green" energy, ignoring the environmental and social impacts of sugarcane monocropping.

The cycle of increasing prices of agricultural commodities in international markets, which started after the crash of the Nasdaq Stock Exchange in 2001 and lasted until the global financial crisis of 2008, coincided with the drive to promote agrofuels (ethanol and agrodiesel) around the world. In Brazil, increasing production of agrofuels served to justify governmental subsidies and marketing policies to support agribusiness, especially soy, sugarcane, palm oil and genetically modified maize. Those policies were rationalized by the idea that agrofuels were a solution to climate change because they could replace fossil fuels.

In the 2000s, agribusiness corporations in Brazil took advantage of negotiations within the World Trade Organization (WTO) to increase market access for export-oriented agricultural commodities. Since the creation of the WTO in 1995, its principal role has been to expand its regulatory power over international trade while promoting a "free market" discourse. The scope of WTO agreements goes beyond issues related to international trade to encompass intellectual property, deregulation of investments and privatization of service sectors. The official line within the WTO about the supposed benefits of ethanol production included the prospect of accessing foreign markets and providing energy security in times of crises. In exchange for increasing export quotas for Brazilian agricultural commodities, the United States and the European Union demanded market access for multinational corporations in key industrial, financial and service sectors, and pressured countries to sign intellectual property agreements.

The expectation of exporting larger amounts of ethanol influenced the territorial expansion of sugarcane plantations in Brazil, which increased from 4.8 to 8.1 million hectares between 2000 and 2011. During that period, the amount of processed sugarcane rose from 257.6 million to 624.9 million tonnes, and ethanol production grew from 11 billion to 27.7 billion litres. Sugarcane production increased by approximately 142 percent between 2000 and 2011, with growth of 138 percent for sugar and of 161 percent for ethanol production during the same period. Both sugarcane yields and the amount of land used to produce sugarcane continued to increase until the 2008 global financial crisis. After that, the main trend was a reduction in productivity while sugarcane plantations continued to expand. In the 2009–10 harvest, sugarcane monocropping increased 9.2 percent, but productivity rose only 2 percent (Mendonça, Pitta and Xavier 2012). Productivity continued to decrease in the following years, and sugarcane production was lower in the 2011–12 harvest year. Due to the decline in ethanol production, in 2011 Brazil had to import maize-based ethanol from the United States.

Until then, sugarcane corporations in Brazil had defended the idea that they could meet the international demand for ethanol. However, the fall in productivity became evident when Brazil had to import ethanol from the United States. This was a key moment that revealed the influence of new mechanisms of speculation in the sector: farmland prices continued to rise after 2008, despite the decrease in agricultural productivity and the price of agricultural commodities on international markets. The disconnect between increasing land prices and decreasing commodity prices revealed the speculative nature of operations in farmland markets by financial corporations. Also, agribusiness's need to continue its territorial expansion contradicts its alleged "efficiency" because it is only able to maintain productivity by appropriating and destroying natural resources, such as land and water.

Financial speculation on the price of farmland is driving the current expansion of agribusiness in Brazil, in which international financial corporations such as TIAA and other pension funds from Europe and Canada play a key role. To start operating in Brazilian farmland markets, TIAA partnered with Cosan, the largest sugarcane corporation in Brazil, to create a rural real estate subsidiary called Radar Propriedades Agrícolas.

Ethanol Production and Financial Speculation on Farmland

The global economic crisis of 2008 altered the profile of agribusiness in Brazil. Foreign corporations acquired several Brazilian companies that had gone into insolvency, or entered into joint ventures with Brazilian companies that remained afloat. To avoid responsibility for unpaid debts, many Brazilian sugarcane plants declared bankruptcy and were able to continue accessing state credit, to roll over debts and avoid paying fines for violations of labour and environmental laws. Another strategy was merging with larger corporations and adopting a new legal name and a new official registration number.

This process led to greater market concentration in the ethanol industry, which agribusiness corporations used as a strategy to increase their share prices as a basis for obtaining new lines of credit and subsidies. A company's ability to acquire debt is directly tied to its size or to the value of its assets, such as land and machinery. During the period of expansion of ethanol production, sugarcane corporations increased their level of mechanization, acquiring new debt to cover the costs of industrial inputs and machinery, which also stimulated the territorial expansion of plantations and financial speculation on farmland. In 2019, the accumulated debt of sugarcane corporations was R$69.2 billion, which was equivalent to about US$20 billion (Bassi 2019).

With preferential access to subsidized credit and other types of state subsidies, Brazilian agribusiness is a major producer of ethanol. In 2010, a joint venture between Cosan (which also partnered with TIAA to operate in farmland markets) and the Dutch oil company Shell created Raízen, the largest producer of ethanol in Brazil. Part of a strategy used by oil corporations to associate themselves with "green energy," this partnership was a major operation, as Raízen had an estimated market value of US$20 billion. Raízen started with an annual production of 2.2 billion litres of ethanol and 4 million tonnes of sugar. The joint venture included parts of major Cosan assets, such as sugar and ethanol plants, ethanol export terminals, retail logistics, pipelines and agricultural land. Shell contributed assets such as fuel distribution, retail and aviation fuel structures. The joint venture also incorporated the distribution network of Exxon (using the Esso brand in Brazil), which had already merged with Cosan in 2008, leaving Raízen with a total of approximately 4,500 gas stations, 550 convenience stores and 54 fuel distribution terminals at airports (Xavier, Pitta and Mendonça 2011).

Cosan was founded in 1936 as a family business in the city of Piracicaba, in the state of São Paulo. For about fifty years, the company had only one sugarcane processing unit. In 1986, it adopted strategies to expand, beginning with the acquisition of three new plants. The company gradually increased its territorial control over farmland as well. This expansion was possible because the government lifted export restrictions on sugar mills in the southcentral region of Brazil by putting an end to the northeastern mills' exclusive access to foreign markets (Leal 2008).

In the 1990s, Cosan started a research project on new types of sugarcane hybrids and developed "very high polarization" sugar, which allowed it to increase its presence in international markets. In 1996, the Brazilian government handed an area that it had previously designated for the construction and operation of an export terminal in the Port of Santos over to Cosan, which resulted in the creation of another subsidiary company called Cosan Portuária. The state concession of a port terminal was a key mechanism for Cosan to operate in foreign markets and to partner with multinational corporations, such as the British sugar group Tate & Lyle, the US-based agribusiness corporation Cargill and the French corporations Tereos and Sucden (Xavier, Pitta and Mendonça 2011).

Especially after 2006, Cosan started to expand sugarcane plantations to the central-western region, establishing plants in the Cerrado biome in the states of Mato Grosso do Sul and Goiás. This territorial expansion was followed by the creation of its rural real estate company, Radar Propriedades Agrícolas, in 2008. Radar acquired farmland for Cosan's sugarcane production but also for leasing to other agribusiness corporations dealing in soy, cotton, maize and eucalyptus, starting a process of speculation with land prices in Brazil. This trend attracted foreign financial corporations such as TIAA, which became a major partner in this business.

One of the effects of the financial crisis was an increasing concentration of capital in the production of ethanol. At that time, since Brazilian sugarcane companies had more difficulty accessing credit, they established joint ventures with foreign corporations, as in the case of Cosan and Shell. In 2009 and 2010, other joint ventures with foreign corporations included British oil company BP partnering with Brazilian companies Tropical BioEnergia, Maeda Group and Santelisa Vale to produce sugarcane in an area of sixty thousand hectares in the state of Goiás; Bunge partnering with the Moema Group, gaining control over 89 percent of the group's sugarcane production, estimated at 15.4 million tonnes per year; and ETH Bioenergia, which was controlled by the Odebrecht group, partnering with Brenco (Companhia Brasileira de Energia Renovável). Brenco's main shareholders included James Wolfensohn (former World Bank president),

Henri Philippe Reichstul (former president of the Brazilian oil company Petrobras) and Vinod Khosla (founder of Sun Microsystems). The newly formed partnership between ETH Bioenergia and Brenco announced a goal of producing three billion litres of ethanol per year with financial support from the BNDES. Odebrecht also partnered with the Japanese company Sojitz to operate five sugarcane plants in the states of São Paulo, Goiás and Mato Grosso do Sul. This conglomerate was involved in the construction of an ethanol pipeline to the Port of Santos.

The participation of foreign corporations in the Brazilian sugarcane industry rose from 1 percent in 2000 to about 25 percent in 2010, especially because of partnerships between agribusiness corporations and other sectors, such as oil, automotive, biotechnology, mineral, infrastructure and financial. A major incentive for these businesses was international market growth for flex-fuel cars. Several foreign groups started to operate in sugar and ethanol production in Brazil, owning more than one hundred plants. Some of these groups were Açúcar e Álcool Fundo de Investimento em Participações (formed by Carlyle, Riverstone, Global Foods, Goldman Sachs, Discovery Capital and DiMaio Ahmad), Abengoa (Spain), Adecoagro (formed by the Soros group), ADM (US), Brazil Ethanol (US), BP (UK), Bunge (US), Cargill (US), Clean Energy (UK), Glencore (Switzerland), Infinity Bio-Energy (UK), Louis Dreyfus (France), Mitsubishi (Japan), Mitsui (Japan), Noble Group (China), Shree Renuka Sugars (India), Syngenta (Switzerland), Sojitz Corporation (Japan), Sucden (France), Kuok (China), Tereos (France) and Umoe (Norway) (Mendonça, Pitta and Xavier 2012).

Access to International Markets and the Role of the State in Promoting Agrofuels

The expansion of sugarcane production in Brazil was supported by a series of government policies aimed at securing bilateral and multilateral export agreements and turning ethanol into a global commodity to be traded on futures markets. However, these goals were not achieved mainly because of a change in public opinion based on research showing the negative environmental and social impacts of expanding sugarcane plantations, such as deforestation and labour law violations. As more research results were published, it became clear that ethanol was not "clean" energy. Another problem was the fact that Brazilian ethanol was not able to provide energy security in international markets, mainly because of the speculative nature of agribusiness and its dependency on credit and financial systems.

In an attempt to meet international requirements to export ethanol, Brazilian sugarcane corporations and agribusiness associations developed certification mechanisms, such as the Better Sugar Cane Initiative by Bonsucro.[2] Similar to other certification schemes used by corporations to improve their image, this is a voluntary process with no independent monitoring of the social and environmental impacts of the sugarcane industry.

Until the 2009–10 harvest and the decline in productivity, Brazil was able to export ethanol to several countries. The largest amount of ethanol exported at that time was to Europe, especially to the Netherlands, the United Kingdom and Switzerland. Other major export markets were the United States, Japan and India (Repórter Brasil 2011). In the European Union, the use of "renewable" fuel was stimulated by Directive 2009/28/CE of May 2009, which required member states to replace 20 percent of their total energy sources and at least 10 percent of transportation energy with agrofuels by 2020. This policy was the main incentive for the Brazilian ethanol lobby to try expanding its access to that market. European Union consumption of agrofuels increased 113.05 percent from 2006 to 2010, jumping from 5.9 million to 12.6 million tonnes. The main source was biodiesel, which rose from 4.1 million to 9.9 million tonnes used during said period. In the United States, the Environmental Protection Agency estimated that to meet the demand for agrofuels, the country would need to increase production from 80 billion litres in 2010 to 136 billion litres in 2022. Brazil has not been able to meet that type of demand. In 2010, the country exported only 1.5 million tonnes of ethanol, which represented a reduction of 42.4 percent compared to the 2008–09 harvest. At that time, the price of ethanol started to increase in comparison to oil prices, becoming less competitive in Brazil and in international markets (Mendonça, Pitta and Xavier 2012).

Even during periods of crisis, the Brazilian government continued to provide subsidized credit to the ethanol industry, which received a R$7.4 billion loan (equivalent to about US$4.3 billion considering the exchange rate at that time) from the BNDES in 2010. This was much higher than the amount of subsidized credit that the BNDES provided to other industries that year: paper, cellulose and extractive industries received R$ 3.1 billion, the mechanical industry R$ 5.3 billion, the metal industry R$ 4.9 billion and the textile and clothing industry R$ 2.1 billion (Mendonça, Pitta and Xavier 2012). To finance these loans with subsidized interest rates, the Brazilian state expanded its debt by selling national treasury bonds on financial markets. The subsidy consisted of the difference between the interest rate paid by the government, based on the official rate of 12 percent at that time, and the interest rate charged by the BNDES, which was 6 percent at that time. When a state bank like the BNDES provides loans with interest rates below market rates, it creates a debt that will have to be covered by taxpayers. In 2009, the year before receiving that large loan, the sugarcane industry had already accumulated a debt of R$40 billion with the BNDES (Ramos 2011).

Most subsidized credit for agribusiness in Brazil is available through public banks, at interest rates that are lower than those the state pays when it offers public debt in the form of government bonds in financial markets in order to attract investments. This state policy is used to promote agricultural exports and gain access to foreign currencies, which allows corporations to obtain loans and rollover debts. According to the 2013–14 Agriculture and Livestock Plan, the amount of public funds allocated to agribusiness through credit mechanisms increased more than fivefold in a decade, jumping from R$27 billion in the 2003–04 harvest to R$136 billion in the 2013–14 harvest (Ministério da Agricultura, Pecuária e Abastecimento 2013).

These credit mechanisms promoted financial speculation because agribusiness corporations used these funds to operate in financial markets, as in the case of sugarcane corporations that received publicly funded loans and used them to speculate on foreign exchange derivatives. Several sugarcane and ethanol plants took advantage of governmental loans at subsidized interest rates to speculate on the appreciation of the Brazilian currency (real) in relation to the US dollar in the years prior to the 2008 economic crisis. But when this trend changed, many sugarcane mills went bankrupt. In 2011, the sector accumulated over R$4 billion in losses in foreign exchange transactions. In January 2012, the Brazilian government freed up R$4 billion in additional subsidized credit for the sugarcane industry, which was to be used specifically for plantation renewal (Mendonça, Pitta and Xavier 2012).

In addition to subsidized credit, during the decade of increasing commodity prices that started in 2001, the Brazilian government provided several types of incentives, such as market security and infrastructure, to the sugarcane industry to attempt to turn ethanol into a commodity traded on international financial markets. The sugarcane industry grew exponentially in Brazil between 2003 and 2008, which is when the number of sugar and ethanol companies increased from 338 to 495. But after 2008, sugarcane corporations had more difficulty accessing credit to pay for previous debts, which led many companies to declare bankruptcy. Between 2008 and 2014, the number of sugar and ethanol companies decreased from 495 to 375 (Pitta 2016).

Sugarcane producers pointed to several cyclical aspects to explain this crisis, mainly relating to climatic factors such as severe rains or prolonged dry seasons. Although these factors can indeed have a negative impact on agricultural production, they are not sufficient to explain the crisis of agribusiness. After 2008, a decrease in sugarcane productivity in Brazil was accompanied by a consistent increase in planted area. This was part of the crisis, as sugarcane corporations appropriated more land and water to try to compensate for losses in productivity. The territorial expansion of plantations also promoted financial speculation on farmland.

Social and Environmental Impacts of Ethanol Production

Before the new cycle of expansion, sugarcane plantations were mostly located in the southcentral and northeastern regions of Brazil. During the 2000s, the new target of expansion was the Cerrado in the central-western region, especially in the states of Mato Grosso do Sul (38.8 percent of the territorial expansion) and Goiás (50.1 percent of territorial expansion) (Mendonça, Pitta and Xavier 2012).

The Cerrado has large river basins and is the most biodiverse savannah in the world. The expansion of sugarcane plantations increased deforestation in the region and also affected the Pantanal and the Amazon by pushing the agricultural frontiers of soy and cattle to the central-northern areas of the country. Environmental destruction in the Cerrado has changed rainfall patterns, causing drought and affecting water levels in rivers that run into the Pantanal and the Amazon, as these biomes are interconnected.

Another impact on the environment and public health is air pollution caused by producers who usually burn the fields before the sugarcane harvest. As described by a local newspaper in the state of Mato Grosso do Sul, "large-scale pollution is visible in several areas and low humidity in the air increases the risk of respiratory diseases" (Dourados Agora 2008). According to Brazil's National Institute for Space Research, during periods of burning fields for the sugarcane harvest, several municipalities declare a state of emergency because air humidity reaches extremely low levels (Ribeiro 2008).

To respond to criticisms about the environmental impacts of burning sugarcane and violations of labour rights, ethanol producers draw attention to mechanization in their sustainability reports, aimed at improving their access to international markets. A main argument for mechanizing sugarcane harvesting is that it does not require the use of fire. However, corporations continue burning fields after mechanization because it increases yields and the level of sucrose. Another reason companies continue to burn sugarcane is because it becomes drier and lighter, which lowers the cost of transporting it from the plantations to the mills.

Burning sugarcane for harvesting releases carbon dioxide (CO_2). Other phases of ethanol production, such as processing, refining, transportation and distribution, also increase CO_2 emissions. Each litre of processed ethanol consumes twelve litres of water, and this amount does not include irrigation in the fields, which consumes even more water. The distillation process of ethanol produces vinasse, which is a type of toxic waste that pollutes the soil, rivers and underground water. Pollution from vinasse is one hundred times higher than domestic sewage. Producing a litre of ethanol generates ten to eighteen litres of vinasse (Ho 2006). Sugarcane producers use it as fertilizer, which has devastating environmental impacts because it is highly corrosive, and it is usually moved from the distilleries into the soil at very high temperatures of 70 to 80 degrees Celsius. When it is dumped on the ground or used as fertilizer, it increases soil acidity and releases CO_2 into the atmosphere (Silva, Griebeler and Borges 2007).

Sugarcane plantations dominate some of the best agricultural lands in Brazil, especially in regions with more infrastructure and large river basins, replacing the food production of small farmers, peasants and Indigenous communities. In the state of Mato Grosso do Sul, sugarcane corporations have been expanding plantations into the territory of the Indigenous Guarani-Kaiowá people, affecting forty-seven thousand residents in an area of about twenty thousand hectares. In 2011, the Raízen corporation (the joint venture between Cosan and Shell) had to sign an agreement with the Brazilian Public Prosecutor's Office to compensate Indigenous communities of Caarapó in Mato Grosso do Sul for planting sugarcane on their land (Mendonça, Pitta and Xavier 2012).

The state of Mato Grosso do Sul is located in the Cerrado and the Pantanal biomes, which are rich in biodiversity and water sources. In recent decades, it has been a main target of agribusiness corporations that are expanding plantations of sugarcane, soy, eucalyptus and genetically modified maize, which is intensifying land concentration and violence against Indigenous Peoples who are displaced from their land. This agricultural system is based on a neocolonial view that promotes the idea that Brazil has large areas of "empty" land and ignores the territorial rights of rural communities. During the period of high demand for ethanol on international markets, from 2003 to 2010, 250 Indigenous people were assassinated in Mato Grosso do Sul, and another 202 Indigenous people were killed elsewhere in Brazil. The number of suicide cases in the state was 176, which represented 83 percent of suicides among Indigenous people in Brazil. Other concerns stemming from the displacement of Indigenous communities are malnutrition, lack of access to health care and death threats against Indigenous leaders who work in defence of their land rights.[3]

When Indigenous communities are surrounded by plantations that use large amounts of chemical inputs, their food production is contaminated. This enables agribusiness corporations to exploit Indigenous people, who are recruited by "headhunters" to work on plantations. Evanildo, an Indigenous community organizer in Mato Grosso do Sul, said that "workers knock themselves out cutting sugarcane and suffer from the impacts of chemical inputs on their health and the environment, which are long-term." He also reported the use of child labour, remembering his own experience:

> It's common to find Indigenous youth working on plantations with fake documents. When I was seventeen, I worked cutting sugarcane and I can still feel the effects of that today. We were housed in plastic tents. I didn't have a contract and we had to pay for all of the equipment and food.

Evanildo explained that prejudice against Indigenous people varies between the colonial image of the "lazy Indian" and the corporate discourse that promotes the idea that they are most "apt" for heavy labour.

Other Indigenous people in the region told similar stories. João started cutting sugarcane when he was sixteen years old. He left his community to work on a sugarcane plantation and only had one day off every forty-five days. In areas where burning sugarcane was prohibited, cutting "raw" cane exposed workers to contact with snakes, scorpions and other insects. The work hours were from 5:30 a.m. to 4:30 p.m., and since the corporation did not pay wages on a regular basis, workers usually had to organize strikes.

Indigenous people in Mato Grosso do Sul are constantly organizing to reoccupy their territories and demand demarcation of their land as a way to stop labour exploitation. Reginaldo, who organized a health clinic in his community, told his story of working on plantations: "The companies deduct the costs of clothing, food, water and equipment from workers' pay. Occupational diseases such as back, shoulder, arm and hand problems are common, as are lung diseases and tuberculosis caused by exposure to pollution and unsanitary lodging conditions."

Pollution of the soil decreases agricultural productivity and so, in order to expand plantations, sugarcane corporations also use small farmers as external suppliers through land use agreements and leasing contracts. These mechanisms stimulate rural real estate speculation, which increases the prices of food and farmland. Small farmers who are contracted as suppliers have to take responsibility for all the impacts on their land, as sugarcane corporations outsource production but control prices, processing and distribution. Ethanol corporations use this outsourcing process to promote their image by claiming the system benefits small farmers and by creating certifications for so-called social fuel.

The payment system is usually determined by the amount of total recoverable sugar (TRS) in each tonne of cane; thus, it depends on the quantity and quality of the raw material. This is a strategy used by sugarcane corporations to manipulate the payment system, because suppliers (including small farmers) do not have access to information about their TRS. Also, the price of TRS is not stable, varying according to the oscillation of sugar and ethanol prices on internal and external markets. Another problem is the fall in productivity levels of sugarcane over time, as well as the oscillation in sugarcane prices, which usually decrease during the harvest time, just before suppliers receive their payment.

Some small farmers who do not have access to appropriate state support have experienced economic difficulties and leased their lands to sugarcane corporations, often getting into debt. Mauro, a small farmer in Mato Grosso do Sul, explained that a sugar plant representative convinced him to grow sugarcane, promising to pay well. Mauro sold part of his cattle to invest in planting sugarcane and to cover the costs of supplies and harvesting, but the plant never paid him. Pedro, another small farmer in the region, had a similar experience:

> I spent money on the crop, fuel and labour and didn't receive anything in return. I ended up in debt. I used to produce manioc, beans, corn and wheat, but because of lack of incentives, I had to lease the land. I also worked as a tractor driver at the plant and had to eat lunch while driving and could not go to the bathroom. It was like slavery.

Labour Exploitation on Sugarcane Plantations

Ethanol production has forced small farmers off their land and generated a dependency on the "sugarcane economy," where only precarious jobs exist in the fields. Large landowners' monopoly over land blocks other economic sectors from developing, generates unemployment, stimulates migration and submits workers to degrading conditions.

Labour exploitation is a part of a structural system on sugarcane plantations in Brazil in which the payment of workers is based on productivity, not hourly work. Payment based on the amount of sugarcane a worker has cut is determined by the mill's scales, and workers have no way to monitor them. In the last few decades, most sugarcane corporations increased mechanization as a way to replace workers and improve their image in relation to labour rights violations, especially to reach international markets. During the 1970s and 1980s, sugarcane producers increased the mechanization of planting and crop treatment (Silva 2002), but the mechanization of the harvest process only became more common in the twenty-first century.

Further industrialization of agriculture has led to growing unemployment in the sugarcane sector. The national rate of mechanization in sugarcane harvesting rose from 18 percent in 1989 to 80 percent in 2014. By that time, 75 percent of sugarcane harvesting had been mechanized in the state of São Paulo, which is the country's largest producer. In the states of Mato Grosso do Sul and Goiás, where plantations expanded during that period, mechanization reached 50 percent (Pitta 2016). Machinery replaced workers by the thousands, causing the number of jobs to drop significantly. In the state of São Paulo, the number of rural workers in 1986 was estimated at 440,000. In 2014, this number had decreased to approximately 94,000 (Baccarin 2014).

Replacing sugarcane cutters with machines increased exploitation and competition among workers who had to meet larger production quotas to keep their jobs. Sugarcane corporations also used mechanization as a strategy to blackmail workers who demanded higher wages and better labour conditions. To avoid responsibility for labour rights, sugarcane corporations contracted temporary workers via intermediary schemes. This system of exploitation included the illegal transportation of migrant workers from different regions of Brazil to the plantations, where they faced contemporary slavery conditions. As they were forced to repay debts incurred for the costs of equipment, housing and food, they received almost no payment for their labour.

Mechanization of sugarcane plantations escalated exploitation, since the quota for sugarcane cutters increased from four tonnes of sugarcane per day in 1980 to approximately ten tonnes in 2006. In the state of São Paulo, workers received about US$1.20 per tonne of sugarcane cut and packed. To receive $220 per month, workers would have to cut an average of ten tonnes of sugarcane per day. Meeting this goal would require swinging their scythe thirty times per minute over eight hours of work per day. New technology used in genetically modified sugarcane makes it lighter and increases labour exploitation: one hundred square metres of regular sugarcane weighs ten tonnes, whereas three hundred square metres of genetically modified sugarcane are needed to reach the same weight (Ramos 2007).

Machine operators in sugarcane plantations also face exploitation, typically working twelve hours a day. In 2012, the Public Prosecutor's Office reported a case where the labour rights of machine operators were violated at a plantation controlled by Raízen. According to the inspectors' report,

> Raízen committed fraud with the clear goal of reducing the costs of the production process. At least ten workers hired by the Marca de Ibaté outsourcing firm had an employment relationship with Raízen. Their contract was terminated with the corporation, which was Cosan at that time, on July 28, 2011, and they were rehired by the outsourcing firm the following day, on July 29, 2011, to carry out the same tasks. This mechanism increases precariousness, as workers' salaries with the outsourcing firm corresponded on average to 63 percent of the salary paid by Raízen.... Workers do not have access to washrooms, a place to have meals, shelter, drinking water and first aid supplies, which are essential in case of accidents. The inspection identified excessively long working days and no breaks. (Jornal de Araraquara 2012)

In 2011, the Ministry of Labour reported a case of slave labour at a mechanized sugarcane plantation:

> Workers who were subjected to a regime analogous to slavery in the mechanized harvesting process have been liberated. In total, thirty-nine workers were rescued. They operated sugarcane-cutting machines on an estate in the city of Goiatuba, Goiás. Their work schedule alternated twenty-four-hour workdays (twenty-seven when one includes the three hours of travel to and from plantations) with a break of twenty-one consecutive hours. At least two accidents caused by fatigue at the wheel were registered. The accidents involved two drivers that had been operating machines for more than twenty hours straight. (RádioAgência NP 2011)

These cases demonstrate that slave labour and degrading working conditions continued in sugarcane plantations after mechanization. In some cases, labour conditions got worse because of the demand on workers to increase productivity to keep their jobs.

The pressure to increase productivity caused the deaths of dozens of sugarcane workers due to exhaustion in the fields during the 2000s, in addition to many reported cases of illnesses and mutilations. Labour exploitation got worse when the demand for ethanol increased on international markets. Between 2004 and 2007, the Ministry of Labour recorded twenty-one deaths of workers in the fields due to exhaustion and generalized cramps throughout their bodies from cutting sugarcane. For that same time, the Ministry of Labour documented an additional 450 deaths of sugarcane workers by other causes, including assassinations, accidents during the precarious transport to the plantations, illnesses such as cardiac arrest and cancer and severe burns from fires in the field. In 2007, the Ministry of Labour recorded three workers' deaths in the sugarcane fields in the state of São Paulo. José Pereira Martins, fifty-two years old, died from a heart attack after cutting sugarcane in the city of Guariba. Twenty-year-old Lourenço Paulino de Souza was found dead at the São José plantation, in Barretos. Adriano de Amaral, thirty-one, died when the water ran out from the hose that he was using to control a fire. Another worker in that incident, forty-four-year-old Ivanildo Gomes, had burns on 44 percent of his body (Mendonça 2012).

During the period of increasing mechanization in sugarcane plantations, between 2003 and 2010, the Pastoral Land Commission documented more than ten thousand cases of workers rescued from slavery conditions. They were not registered workers and were living in precarious shelters. They had no protective equipment, an inadequate water and food supply and no access to bathrooms. Workers had to pay for their equipment, such as boots and machetes, and in cases of accidents, they did not receive medical treatment. From 2003 to 2006, sugarcane corporations were responsible for 10 percent of total cases of slave labour in Brazil, or 1,605 cases. This percentage increased in the following years to 51 percent in 2007, or 3,060 cases; 48 percent in 2008, or 2,553 cases; 45 percent in 2009, or 1,911 cases; and 18 percent in 2010, or 535 cases.[4]

In 2006, the Attorney General's Office cited seventy-four plantations in the state of São Paulo, and all of them were charged. In March 2007, the Ministry of Labour rescued 288 workers in slave-like conditions at six plantations in the state of São Paulo. In another operation carried out in March of that year, a group from the Regional Labour Precinct (Delegacia Regional do Trabalho) of Mato Grosso do Sul rescued 409 workers, including 150 Indigenous people, in sugarcane fields. In June 2007, the Ministry of Labour freed 1,108 workers in slavery conditions in sugarcane plantations in the state of Pará in the Amazon region. The workers received less than

R$10 (about US$5, according to the exchange rate at that time) per month, and the illegal deductions from workers' wages by the company consumed almost the entire amount. The inspectors reported that the food supplied to the workers was rotten, and they suffered from nausea and diarrhea. Their drinking water was filthy, and it was the same water used for irrigation in the fields. The workers' shelter was very crowded and had an open sewer inside. The majority of workers were migrants from the states of Maranhão and Piauí, but the company did not provide transportation for them to return home (Mendonça 2012).

These types of labour violations were found on farms operated by large corporations such as Cosan. In June 2007, an inspection by the Ministry of Labour found forty-two workers who were facing conditions comparable to slavery in a Cosan mill in the state of São Paulo. In 2008, other inspections found several violations of labour laws in eighteen Cosan plants. The public prosecutor described some of these violations as "lack of drinking water and toilets at the workplace, lack of protective equipment and lack of appropriate eating conditions." In March 2010, an inspection by the Ministry of Labour found violations of labour laws at another Cosan plant called Gaza, where 350 workers described a lack of protective equipment, adequate tools, sanitary facilities, drinking water and access to basic medical care and first aid. They also reported dangerous working conditions, including with the transportation used, which was associated with long working hours to increase productivity. As a result, Cosan had to sign two legal agreements with the Public Prosecutor's Office and pay fines of R$2.5 million and R$900,000 for violating labour laws (Mendonça, Pitta and Xavier 2014).

Most sugarcane cutters are men, but companies also hire women for manual cutting and planting. Their payment is based on productivity, and when planting they have to cover a very large area, averaging 750 square metres, per day to receive R$9 (US$5) in wages. Women farmworkers described how exploitation is a historical characteristic in sugarcane plantations in Brazil.[5] "I started working when I was eleven years old to help my mother in the fields when she was pregnant. My mother got very sick and died when she was fifty-nine. I'm forty-two now and I think the same will happen to me," said Maria Souza from the state of Pernambuco. In the state of São Paulo, Lusiane dos Santos described a similar situation: "I'm thirty-eight years old and I started cutting sugarcane when I was twenty. I had to stop going to school because my father left us and my mother sent me to work."

Carlita da Costa, president of the Cosmópolis Rural Workers Union in the state of São Paulo, has been organizing farmworkers, especially women, in a sector dominated by men. She started cutting sugarcane at a young age to support her three children, and she knows that workers need to demand structural changes to overcome poverty and oppression:

> It's common to hear people's coughs and screams in the cane fields. We have to inhale pesticides and the ash from burned cane. Once I fell and felt the taste of blood in my mouth. I broke my arm and could not work anymore. I have lung problems and feel sick from that horrible work. I realized that cane cutting was killing me.

Agribusiness's monopoly over land restricts peasants' livelihood options and, as a result, they become more vulnerable to labour exploitation. Many men from rural areas migrate to different regions in the country, looking for seasonal jobs at plantations or construction, and some never return to their families. For women, it is more difficult to find an alternative, and so they usually stay home, taking on the responsibility of caring for their children and elderly parents. But some women also migrate in search of jobs, as in the case of Ana Célia:

> I'm twenty-four and I came from Pernambuco to work in São Paulo. The company only pays for fifty kilos of sugarcane a day, even when we cut sixty kilos. My whole body hurts. I need to leave this job because I'm getting sick. The cost of rent, water and electricity is very high, and after paying for everything, there is nothing left from my salary.

Edite Rodrigues told a similar story:

> I'm thirty-one and I came from the state of Minas Gerais to work in São Paulo. I have three kids and need to support them, but I can't wait to leave this job. At the end of the day, my body is broken, and I feel like throwing up. But the next day, we have to start all over again. The pollution from burning sugarcane is horrible for my lungs, not to mention the effects of pesticides. There is no fixed wage. It depends on how much sugarcane we cut. For women, it's much worse than for men because they give us the worst jobs for less pay. We depend on meal vouchers, or we go hungry.

Odete Mendes, who works at a plantation in São Paulo, said that her salary only covered rent for a very small room and was not enough for other expenses: "I cannot stay in this job. It's very hard. Once I broke my arm. I constantly feel a lot of pain in my hands, my lungs suffocate and sometimes I think I will die in the fields."

Women farmworkers advocate for regular working hours, equal pay, maternity leave, health care, childcare and social benefits. They face a dual situation of oppression because they are responsible for household labour and for providing for their families. Ivanusa Ribeiro, a worker in the state of Pernambuco, explained: "I wake up at two in the morning to start working at 4 a.m., and I only stop at 3 p.m. After getting home, I still have a lot of work to do, cleaning the house, cooking for my kids and my husband." She said this situation will only change if the government gives more incentives for agrarian reform and for small farmers to produce food. She also said she sees the need for an education system that is meaningful to women in the countryside.

Rural Women and Grassroots Feminism

Rural women's resistance is crucial to dealing with the simultaneous economic, ecological and food crises. Women face specific challenges in times of crisis, since they usually have the main responsibility for social tasks in their households, such as providing food and health care. Neoliberal policies that cut governmental support for social programs and inflation in food prices mean an extra burden for working women. In addition, the displacement of rural communities forces women into the worst jobs on plantations and in urban areas.

Women's movements that are part of La Vía Campesina represent 182 rural organizations from 81 countries, including small farmers, pastoralists, fisherfolk, peasant and Indigenous people who advocate for collective land rights, common use of natural resources and an agricultural system based on ecological food production. They are developing a grassroots feminist political analysis and concrete practices to advance social transformation based on new gender relations. Some of their priorities are stopping violence against women and building food sovereignty. "The patriarchal system continues to grow throughout the entire world, violating our territories, our bodies and our minds," says the declaration of the 2017 La Vía Campesina Women's Assembly (La Vía Campesina 2017).

This declaration denounces the major impacts of agribusiness on rural communities, such as displacement, migration, violence, militarization, repression and climate change: "In this context, we women are increasingly bearing the weight of producing goods and food. However, our work continues to be made invisible and our care work is neither valued, supported, nor collectively or socially assumed, thereby increasing our burden of work and restricting our full participation" (La Vía Campesina 2017).

Women peasants and farmworkers are responsible for the production of more than 50 percent of the world's food, but women own less than 2 percent of farmland and represent 70 percent of people facing hunger, malnutrition and food insecurity globally (Monsalve 2015). The production of food for subsistence and for local markets is frequently ignored in official economic data despite its central role in income generation, economic development, employment and food security in rural areas.

For women in rural communities, a main challenge to achieving food sovereignty is lack of control over economic resources and access to land. Women's movements in the countryside advocate to have land titles in their names even if they are not the head of their households. A serious risk for women in rural communities is displacement due to pressure and violence from state agents and private militia groups. Armed conflicts, militarization and repression against rural communities frequently involve control over land, water, mining and other natural sources.

The expansion of agribusiness violates the fundamental human right of access to clean water. The pollution of water sources and the privatization of water services affect women, in particular, who are often responsible for providing water in their households. Speculation on agricultural commodities increases the price of food, which has a disproportionate impact on low-income women, who spend a larger percentage of their income on basic needs. Women usually take the responsibility for providing food and administering the food budget in their households.

Facing these challenges, women's movements demand the right to land, housing, inheritance, educational opportunities, equal representation in decision-making and recognition of their diversity and distinct forms of land tenure systems, including protection of cultural rights of Indigenous communities. Rural women's organizations demand support for small-scale agriculture and women's cooperatives, as well as the right to choose what type of agricultural system they prioritize. This includes inputs and technical assistance based on ecological practices, which determines not only access to food but the quality of the food produced. Governments need to provide special lines of credit and subsidies that prioritize small farmers who produce healthy food for local markets as well as other key resources such as transportation and energy. Women's organizations also demand that governments implement legislation to guarantee environmental protection for biodiversity and water sources.

In addition to grassroots organizing, women's rural movements have advocated for the development of human rights mechanisms to protect the right to food and land. For example, the UN Committee on the Elimination of

Discrimination Against Women (CEDAW), the UN Committee on Economic, Social and Cultural Rights, the UN Food and Agriculture Organization and UN Special Rapporteurs have established standards and recommended human rights protection for rural women. Multiple UN Special Rapporteurs have addressed land-related human rights issues relevant to women.[6] CEDAW's (2016) recommendation on the rights of rural women establishes women's rights to productive resources including land use, ownership and inheritance. States must guarantee the universal right to food by means of concrete actions and measures that protect vulnerable social groups and provide the means necessary for them to have permanent access to healthy food. The Food and Agriculture Organization's Voluntary Guidelines on the Responsible Governance of Tenure of Land, Fisheries and Forests in the Context of National Food Security recognizes the vulnerability of rural women and girls who face displacement as a result of land-grabbing (FIAN International 2011).

The UN Declaration on the Rights of Indigenous Peoples establishes protection against dispossession of land, territories and natural resources. It also establishes procedural protections about the way decisions around land transfers are made in the form of the right to free, prior and informed consent. The UN Declaration on the Rights of Peasants and Other People Working in Rural Areas is the result of rural movements' organizing in defence of gender equality and for international recognition of their right to land, economic and natural resources, ecological agriculture, seeds, water, health care and food sovereignty (La Vía Campesina 2021b).

An important international norm on the right to food is Article 11 of the International Convention on Economic, Social and Cultural Rights. According to this human rights mechanism, hunger should be eliminated, and communities should have permanent access to adequate food, both quantitatively and qualitatively. The Convention establishes the principles of nonregression and nondiscrimination and thus states have the obligation to respect, protect and guarantee the right to food. States cannot obstruct or impede access to food, including in the case of displacement of rural communities from their lands.

Looking at the Past to Change the Future

The production of agrofuels by agribusiness is based on the same historical elements that characterized colonization: exploitation of territory, labour and economic resources. During colonial times, sugar was the main export commodity from Brazil to Europe. Brazil started to produce ethanol in the 1970s during the global oil crisis. The National Ethanol Program

(Proálcool), in place from 1975 to 1990, was a key mechanism for the industrialization of agriculture and the development of technology for vehicles that run on ethanol. The Brazilian government provided subsidized credit to the sugar-energy sector by increasing the country's foreign debt. However, in the 1980s, this system collapsed as a consequence of the debt crisis.

The global economic crisis in the late 1970s caused exchange rate fluctuations and an increase in interest rates on foreign loans to Latin American countries, resulting in the "lost decade" of the 1980s. This led to the Mexican moratorium on debt servicing in 1983. That same year, Brazil took out a loan from the International Monetary Fund for the first time. In 1986, debt service payments amounted to nearly 96 percent of Brazil's export revenue (Oliveira 1998), and the country announced a moratorium of its own. During that period, the Brazilian government justified establishing extensive, mechanized agriculture as a priority for state support by arguing it was necessary to pay off the country's foreign debt and to ensure a positive balance of trade. Dependency on imports of industrial supplies for agriculture, however, increased deficits in the trade balance (Mendonça 2018).

The concentration of the agricultural supplies market in the hands of transnational corporations, as well as their monopoly over commodity trading, was consolidated primarily at the time when the US dollar was adopted as the international reserve currency. This policy increased the financial availability of international credit systems. In Brazil, this period was marked by the military dictatorship (1964–85), during which a major influx of financial capital and industrial imports intensified the industrialization of agriculture.

From 1975 to 1990, the National Ethanol Program allocated more than US$7 billion in public subsidies to support the production of ethanol from sugarcane. This policy also provided state support for mechanization and infrastructure, transportation and the commercialization of ethanol. The mechanization of sugarcane production occurred at the same time as the escalation in Brazil's foreign debt, which jumped from US$3.8 billion in 1968 to US$12.6 billion in 1973, as the military regime offered large subsidies for agribusiness (Pitta 2011).

Brazil renegotiated its external debt in 1994 through an agreement called the Brady Plan. In the implementation of the plan, the government created state debt in the form of bonds that could be traded on financial markets, which resulted in the securitization of credit. Most countries use this financial mechanism in state budgets, generating the impression of economic growth even in times of crises. The result of those policies was financial and environmental deregulation that benefited private monopolies.

While neoliberal ideology defends minimal state participation in economic policy, governments continue to play a central role in transferring public resources to the private sector. The so-called minimal state has never existed for agribusiness corporations. The second wave of major governmental support for ethanol production in Brazil started in 2004. In 2006, more than 425 million tonnes of sugarcane were produced on six million hectares of land, and the country became the largest global producer of ethanol, reaching 17.4 billion litres that year (Mendonça, Melo and Junior 2007). Taking advantage of international concern about climate change, agribusiness and oil corporations continued to receive state support to produce agrofuels.

This context started to change in 2008 with the global food crisis, when the international price of maize rose by 80 percent. Export demand to the United States caused a price surge of 100 percent for tortillas in Mexico, which is the principal food source in the country. In China, foreseeing a food supply problem, the government prohibited maize-based ethanol production. The global demand for agrofuels caused a general increase in food prices because high maize prices inflated the cost of grains for human consumption and for animal rations.

To meet demand in the United States, which produces ethanol from genetically modified maize, 132 billion litres of ethanol would be needed each year. Production of such a large amount would consume the country's entire annual production of maize, about 268 million tonnes, and would still require the country to import close to 110 million tonnes of maize, which was the equivalent of the total annual production in Brazil in 2007 (Mendonça, Melo and Junior 2007). In addition to the risk of genetically modified maize contaminating food production, another concern was that the energy sources for ethanol factories in the United States were coal and gas, which would generate even more carbon emissions.

By the end of the 2000s, it became clear that large-scale production of agrofuels presented a risk for food sovereignty and climate change because it caused land use change by replacing food production with commodity plantations. In the case of soy produced for agrodiesel, major impacts are deforestation and pollution from chemical inputs and agricultural machinery. The case of palm oil is similar. It is known as "the diesel of deforestation" because it has caused large-scale devastation of forests in several countries, such as Colombia, Ecuador, Indonesia and Malaysia. The "second generation" agrofuels, developed from cellulose material and genetically modified eucalyptus plantations, also cause environmental destruction and consume large amounts of water.

Currently, the global production of agrofuels continues to present a risk, which is escalated by growing monopolies over land. In 2020, the international production of agrofuels for transportation was estimated at 144 billion litres, with the largest market percentage represented by ethanol produced in the United States and Brazil (IEA 2020). At the same time, world hunger continues to be a major result of the agribusiness system, as more than 800 million people do not have regular access to food (FAO, IFAD, UNICEF, WFP and WHO 2021). In Brazil, 55.2 percent of households face food insecurity and 9 percent face hunger. From 2018 to 2021, out of a total population of 211.7 million, 116.7 million Brazilians did not have regular access to food and 19 million faced hunger. Since 2018, hunger has increased by 27.6 percent in Brazil (Rede Brasileira de Pesquisa em Soberania e Segurança Alimentar 2021).

Conclusion

Historical cycles of crises reveal that agribusiness's growth has been dependent on access to state subsidies. The study of different aspects of agribusiness — from social, political, economic and historical perspectives — in this book reveals that its main "products" are environmental destruction, debt and economic instability, as in the case of financial speculation in rural land markets. Further, the "competitiveness" of Brazilian ethanol on foreign markets is based on labour exploitation, the appropriation of natural resources and massive amounts of public funds.

The current climate crisis demonstrates that no single source of energy is capable of meeting global demand. The alternative is to implement structural changes to prioritize diversified local energy sources and ecological food systems. Grassroots organizations defend agrarian reform and food sovereignty, which require state support for food production in local markets. In Brazil, agrarian reform is a historical demand of rural movements to change the systemic economic inequality caused by land concentration.

The largest rural organization in Brazil is the Landless Workers' Movement (Movimento dos Trabalhadores Rurais Sem Terra, MST), which was founded in 1984 by organizing land occupations in response to inequality in the countryside. Currently, the MST is present in twenty-four Brazilian states and is made up of 450,000 families who live in agrarian reform communities and 90,000 families who are in land occupations demanding agrarian reform. Over the years, it has built two thousand rural schools and forty educational centres, including the Florestan Fernandes National School. The MST has organized over three hundred cooperatives to promote agroecology and is the largest producer of organic rice in Latin America. In 2020, as a response to the Covid-19 pandemic, it distributed over 3,100 tonnes of food to low-income families in urban areas. The movement is also organizing a national campaign to plant 100 million trees in ten years to recover ecosystems and natural springs (Mafort 2020).

The MST coordinates its actions with other rural movements from La Vía Campesina to expand the territorial scope of agroecology based on the culture and knowledge of peasant and Indigenous communities in different countries. A key element in this process is to preserve seeds and build food sovereignty by sharing experiences and promoting grassroots education. Francisca Rodriguez from La Vía Campesina explained that "agrofuels are a false solution to climate change. We must denounce this destructive project to defend our land and stimulate a profound discussion about the current systems of food and energy production" (La Vía Campesina 2021a).

Rural social movements in Brazil and around the world have been building sophisticated analyses and practices to resist the destructive impacts of agribusiness and to expand agroecology. The different approaches used in this book, including historical research, theoretical investigation and fieldwork, originate from a need to understand the political economy of agribusiness from a critical perspective, as a contribution to movement building on key global issues related to land, food, water and climate.

Notes

1. Agribusiness corporations adopted the term "biofuels" but, because "bio" means life, social movements use "agrofuels" to more accurately describe the impacts of this production system.
2. Information on the certification scheme is available on the Bonsucro website <bonsucro.com>.
3. Data compiled from a report series by Conselho Indigenista Missionário (2003–10).
4. Data compiled from a series of reports by Comissão Pastoral da Terra from 2003 to 2010.
5. Original interviews in Portuguese with women farmworkers were published in Mendonça 2012.
6. For example, the Special Rapporteur on the right to food and the Special Rapporteur on adequate housing as a component of the right to an adequate standard of living. See United Nations (2007).

References

Amin, Samir. 1977. "O capitalismo e a renda fundiária." In *A questão agrária e o capitalismo*, eds. Samir Amin and Kostas Vergopolous. Rio de Janeiro: Paz e Terra.

Associação de Advogados de Trabalhadores Rurais, GRAIN, and Rede Social de Justiça e Direitos Humanos. 2020. *TIAA and Harvard's Brazilian farm deals judged illegal as fires rage on their properties in the biodiverse Cerrado*, December 2020. <social.org.br/files/pdf/Land_grabbing_in_Brazil_EN.pdf>.

Austin, James E. 1974. *Agribusiness in Latin America*. New York: Praeger.

Baccarin, José Giacomo. 2014. *Ocupação formal no setor sucroalcooleiro em São Paulo*. Jaboticabal: UNESP.

Barbosa, Altair Sales. 2008. "Cerrado: biodiversidade e pluralidade." *Cerrado: Do científico ao poético* (blog), November 8. <altairsalesbarbosa.blogspot.com.br/2008>.

Bassi, Bruno Stankevicius. 2019. "Sozinha, dívida do setor sucroenergético cobre metade do déficit primário." *De olho nos ruralistas*, June 27. <https://deolhonosruralistas.com.br/2019/06/27/sozinha-divida-do-setor-sucroenergetico-cobre-metade-do-deficit-primario/>.

Belluzzo, Luiz Gonzaga. 2012. *O capital e suas metamorfoses*. São Paulo: Editora UNESP.

Borges, Thais, and Sue Branford. 2020. "Rapid deforestation of Brazilian Amazon could bring next pandemic: Experts." *Mongabay*, April 15. <news.mongabay.com/2020/04/rapid-deforestation-of-brazilian-amazon-could-bring-next-pandemic-experts/>.

____. 1964. *The Meaning of the Twentieth Century: The Great Transition*. New York: Harper & Row.

Bowman, Emma. 2021. "Amazon deforestation in Brazil hits its worst level in 15 years." NPR, November 19. <npr.org/2021/11/19/1057245837/brazil-amazon-rainforest-worst-deforestation-rate>.

Burbach, Roger, and Patricia Flynn. 1980. *Agribusiness in the Americas*. New York: Monthly Review Press.

Castro, A.M. Gomes, S.M. Valle Lima, and C.M.P. Neves Cristo. 2002. *Cadeia Produtiva: Marco Conceitual para Apoiar a Prospecção Tecnológica*. Brasilia: Ministério da Indústria.

CEDAW. 2016. *General Recommendation No. 34 on the Rights of Rural Women.* CEDAW/C/GC/34, March 7. <tbinternet.ohchr.org/Treaties/CEDAW/Shared%20 Documents/1_Global/INT_CEDAW_GEC_7933_E.pdf>.

Chaidez, Alexandra A. 2019. "As the Amazon burns, students call on Harvard to divest from farmland holdings." *The Harvard Crimson*, August 29. <thecrimson. com/article/2019/8/29/amazon-fires-divestment/>.

Chaidez, Alexandra A., and Meena Venkataramanan. 2019. "Divest Harvard holds protest about university's Brazilian land ownership." *The Harvard Crimson*, October 22. <thecrimson.com/article/2019/10/22/hmc-divest-protest/>.

Chayanov, Alexander. 1974. *La organización de la unidad económica campesina.* Buenos Aires: Ediciones Nueva Visión.

Chesnais, François. 2005. *A finança mundializada.* São Paulo: Boitempo Editorial.

Cochrane, Willard W. 1993. *The Development of American Agriculture: A Historical Analysis.* Minneapolis: University of Minnesota Press.

Comissão Pastoral da Terra. 2003–2010. *Conflitos no campo – Brasil.* Report series: 2003–2010. <cptnacional.org.br/index.php/publicacoes-2/conflitos-no-campo-brasil>.

Conselho Indigenista Missionário. 2003–2010. *Observatório-da-violências contra os Povos Indígenas no Brasil.* Report series: 2003–2010. <cimi.org.br/observatorio-da-violencia/edicoes-anteriores/>.

Cramer, Gail L., Clarence W. Jensen, and Douglas DeWitt Southgate. 2001. *Agricultural Economics and Agribusiness.* New York: John Wiley.

Davis, John H., and Ray A. Goldberg. 1957. *A Concept of Agribusiness.* Boston: Harvard University Graduate School of Business Administration.

Davis, John Herbert, and Kenneth Hinshaw. 1957. *Farmer in a Business Suit.* New York: Simon and Schuster.

Delgado, Guilherme C. 2012. *Do capital financeiro na agricultura à economia do agronegócio: Mudanças cíclicas em meio século (1965–2012).* Porto Alegre: Editora da UFRGS.

____. 1985. *Capital financeiro e agricultura no Brasil: 1965–1985.* Campinas: Editora da UNICAMP/Ícone.

Dourados Agora. 2008. "Mesmo proibidas, começam queimadas de cana em Dourados." July 7. <douradosagora.com.br/2008/07/07/mesmo-proibidas-queimadas-da-cana-comecam-em-dourados/>.

ETC Group. 2009. *Who Will Feed Us? Questions for the Food and Climate Crises.* Ottawa: ETC Group.

FAO, IFAD, UNICEF, WFP, and WHO. 2021. *The State of Food Security and Nutrition in the World 2021.* Rome: FAO. <fao.org/3/cb4474en/cb4474en.pdf>.

Favero, Celso A. 1996. "O Mercosul e a reestruturação da agricultura: As 'filières' de cereais e a exclusão social." *Cadernos de Ciência & Tecnologia*, 13, 3.

FIAN International. 2011. "CSO's Proposals for the FAO Guidelines on Responsible Governance of Land and Natural Resources Tenure." March 28.

França, Caio Galvão de, Mauro Eduardo del Grossi, and Vicente P.M. de Azevedo Marques. 2009. *Family Farming and the 2006 Brazilian Agriculture/ Livestock Census.* Brasília: Núcleo de Estudos Agrários e Desenvolvimento Rural do Ministério do Desenvolvimento Agrário. <repositorio.unb.br/

handle/10482/14747>.

Friends of the Earth US, GRAIN, National Family Farm Coalition, and Rede Social de Justiça e Direitos Humanos. 2019. "Harvard and TIAA's farmland grab in Brazil goes up in smoke." October 17. <foe-us.medium.com/harvard-and-tiaas-farmland-grab-in-brazil-goes-up-in-smoke-52dbfe57debf>.

Goldberg, Ray A. 1985. "Introduction." *Agribusiness: An International Journal*, 1, 1 (Spring).

____. 1974. *Agribusiness Management for Developing Countries — Latin America.* Cambridge: Ballinger Publishing.

Goldberg, Ray A., Kermit Molyneaux Bird, and Henry B. Arthur. 1968. *The Technological Front in the Food and Fiber Economy.* Washington, DC: National Advisory Commission on Food and Fiber.

Goodman, David, et al. 1987. *From Farming to Biotechnology: A Theory of Agro-Industrial Development.* Oxford: Basil Blackwell.

Graham, Laura R., and Meena Khandelwal. 2021. "University of Iowa faculty demand TIAA accountability." *The Gazette*, June 2. <thegazette.com/opinion/university-of-iowa-faculty-demand-tiaa-accountability/>.

GRAIN, and Rede Social de Justiça e Direitos Humanos. 2018. *Harvard's Billion-Dollar Farmland Fiasco,* August. <social.org.br/files/pdf/EN_FINAL_PDF_Harvard.pdf>.

Guardian. 2022. "Brazil: Deforestation jumps in world's largest savanna as scientists raise alarm." January 3. <theguardian.com/world/2022/jan/03/brazil-deforestation-cerrado-scientists-alarm>.

Guimarães, Alberto Passos. 2009. "Formação da pequena propriedade: Intrusos e posseiros (1963)." In *Camponeses Brasileiros*, eds. Clifford Andrew Welch et al., Vol. 1. São Paulo: Editora UNESP.

____. 1978. *A crise agrária*. Rio de Janeiro: Paz e Terra.

Hampe, Edward C., Merle Witteberg, and Lilian Edds. 1980. *The Food Industry: Lifeline of America.* Ithaca: Cornell University.

Ho, Mae-Wan. 2006. *Biofuels: Biodevastation, Hunger & False Carbon Credits.* London: Institute of Science in Society.

Hobsbawm, Eric J. 1984. *História do marxismo*, Vol. 4. Rio de Janeiro: Paz e Terra.

Hodge, Helena N., Todd Merrifield, and Steven Gorelick. 2002. *Bringing the Food Economy Home: Local Alternatives to Global Agribusiness.* London: Zed Books.

Instituto Brasileiro de Geografia e Estatística. 2006. *Censo agropecuário 2006.* Rio de Janeiro: IBGE. <biblioteca.ibge.gov.br/visualizacao/periodicos/51/agro_2006.pdf>.

IEA. 2020. *Renewables 2020.* <https://iea.blob.core.windows.net/assets/1a24f1fe-c971-4c25-964a-57d0f31eb97b/Renewables_2020-PDF.pdf>.

Jank, Marcos Sawaya. 2005. "Agronegócio versus agricultura familiar?" *O Estado de São Paulo*, May 7.

Jornal de Araraquara. 2012. "Raízen (antiga Cosan) é Processada pelo MPT." April 21.

Kageyama, Angela. 1987. *O novo padrão agrícola brasileiro: Do complexo rural aos complexos agro-industriais.* Campinas: UNICAMP.

Kautsky, Karl. 1968. *A questão agrária* [The agrarian question]. Rio de Janeiro: Editora Laemmert.

Kloppenburg, Jack R. 1988. *First the Seed: The Political Economy of Plant Biotechnology*. Cambridge: Cambridge University Press.

Konder, Leandro. 2009. *A derrota da dialética* [The defeat of dialectics]. São Paulo: Expressão Popular.

La Vía Campesina. 2021a. "La Vía Campesina: Construction of shared knowledge on peasant seeds." December 9. <viacampesina.org/en/la-via-campesina-launches-training-modules-on-peasant-seeds/>.

____. 2021b. "Training modules: UN Declaration on Rights of Peasants and Other People Working in Rural Areas (UNDROP)." December 16. <https://viacampesina.org/en/training-modules-un-declaration-on-rights-of-peasants-and-other-people-working-in-rural-areas-undrop/>.

____. 2017. "V Women's Assembly, La Vía Campesina, Declaration." <viacampesina.org/en/vii-international-conference-womens-assembly-declaration/>.

Leal, H.M.Q. 2008. "O grupo Cosan em questão: Formação, expansão e reprodução do capital canavieiro no interior paulista." In *Simpósio de Pós-graduação em Geografia do Estado de São Paulo*. Rio Claro: Unesp.

Lefebvre, Henri. 2008. *Critique of Everyday Life*, Volume II, London: Verso.

Lukács, Georg. 2003. *História e consciência de classe*. São Paulo: Martins Fontes.

Luxemburg, Rosa. 1985. *A acumulação do capital*. São Paulo: Editora Abril Cultural.

Mafort, Kelli. 2020. "O MST e a mobilização social em tempos de pandemia." In *Direitos humanos no Brasil 2020*, eds. Daniela Stefano and Maria Luisa Mendonça. São Paulo: Outras Expressões. <social.org.br/livros-books/livros-direitos-humanos-no-brasil/250-relatorio-direitos-humanos-2020>.

Martins, Mônica Dias. 2008. *Açúcar no Sertão: A ofensiva capitalista no Nordeste do Brasil*. São Paulo: Annablume.

Marx, Karl. 1983–1985. *Capital: A Critique of Political Economy*, Vols. 1, 2 and 3. São Paulo: Abril Cultural.

____. 1977. *Capital*, Vol. 1. New York: Vintage Books.

McDonald, Michael. 2020. "Harvard spins off natural resources team, to remain partner." *Bloomberg*, October 8. <https://farmlandgrab.org/29894>.

McMichael, Philip. 2000. "Global food politics." In *Hungry for Profit: The Agribusiness Threat to Farmers, Food, and the Environment*, eds. Fred Magdoff, John Bellamy Foster and Frederick H. Buttel. New York: Monthly Review Press.

Mendonça, Maria Luisa. 2018. *Economia política do agronegócio*. São Paulo: Editora Annablume.

____. 2015. "A crise permanente do agronegócio." In *Direitos humanos no Brasil 2015: Relatório da rede social de justiça e direitos humanos*, eds. Daniela Stefano and Maria Luisa Mendonça. São Paulo: Rede Social de Justiça e Direitos Humanos and Editora Expressão Popular Ltda.

____. 2012. *Monopólio da terra no Brasil: Impactos da expansão de monocultivos para a produção de agrocombustíveis*. São Paulo: Rede Social de Justiça e Direitos Humanos e Comissão Pastoral da Terra. <social.org.br/pub/revistas-portugues/80-revista-monopolio-da-terra-no-brasil2>.

Mendonça, Maria Luisa, Marluce Melo and Plácido Junior. 2007. *Agroenergy, Myths and Impacts in Latin America*. Recife: Comissão Pastoral da Terra and São Paulo: Rede Social de Justiça e Direitos Humanos. <social.org.br/pub/booklets-

english/85-agroenergy-myths-and-impacts-in-latin-america>.

Mendonça, Maria Luisa, Fábio T. Pitta, and Carlos V. Xavier. 2014. *Transnational Corporations and Agrofuels Production in Brazil*. São Paulo: Editora Outras Expressões.

____. 2012. *The Sugarcane Industry and the Global Economic Crisis*. São Paulo: Editora Outras Expressões.

Ministério da Agricultura, Pecuária e Abastecimento. 2021. "Agricultura familiar." June 22. <https://www.gov.br/agricultura/pt-br/assuntos/politica-agricola/plano-safra/2021-2022/agricultura-familiar>.

____. 2020. "Agricultura familiar." May 4, 2020. <https://www.gov.br/agricultura/pt-br/assuntos/agricultura-familiar/agricultura-familiar-1>.

____. 2013. *Plano agrícola e pecuário 2013–2014*. Brasilia: MAPA. <www.gov.br/agricultura/pt-br/assuntos/politica-agricola/todas-publicacoes-de-politica-agricola/plano-agricola-pecuario/plano-agricola-e-pecuario-2013-2014.pdf/view>.

Ministério do Meio Ambiente. 2006. *Plano Nacional de Recursos Hídricos: Panorama e estado dos recursos hídricos do Brasil*, Vol. 1. Brasília.

Mitidiero Junior, Marco Antonio, and Yamila Goldfarb. 2021. *O agro não é tech, o agro não é pop e muito menos tudo*. São Paulo: Friedrich Ebert Stiftung and Associação Brasileira de Reforma Agrária. <library.fes.de/pdf-files/bueros/brasilien/18319-20211027.pdf>.

Monsalve Suárez, Sofia. 2015. "The right to land and other natural resources in the United Nations Declaration on the Rights of Peasants and Other People Working in Rural Areas." *FIAN International Briefing*. Geneva: FIAN International.

Müller, Geraldo. 1989. *Complexo agroindustrial e modernização agrária*. São Paulo: Editora Hucitec.

Oliveira, Ariovaldo U. 1998. "A inserção do Brasil no capitalismo monopolista mundial." In *Geografia do Brasil*, ed. Jurandyr Ross. São Paulo: EDUSP.

Paoliello, Renata M. 1992. *Posse da terra e conflitos sociais no campo*. Campinas: PPGAS/UNICAMP.

Perelman, Michael. 1979. *Farming for Profit in a Hungry World*. Montclair: Allanheld, Osmun Publishers.

Pesquisa Fapesp. n.d. "Incêndios no Pantanal mataram 17 milhões de animais." <https://revistapesquisa.fapesp.br/incendios-no-pantanal-mataram-17-milhoes-de-animais/>.

Pitta, Fábio T. 2016. "As transformações na reprodução fictícia do capital na agroindústria canavieira paulista: do Proálcool à crise de 2008." Doctoral dissertation, University of São Paulo. <teses.usp.br/teses/disponiveis/8/8136/tde-10052016-140701/publico/2016_FabioTeixeiraPitta_VCorr.pdf>.

____. 2011. "Modernização retardatária e agroindústria sucroalcooleira paulista: o Proálcool como reprodução fictícia do capital em crise." Master's dissertation, University of São Paulo. <teses.usp.br/teses/disponiveis/8/8136/tde-20102011-110312/pt-br.php>.

Pitta, Fábio T., Gerardo Cerdas, and Maria Luisa Mendonça. 2018. *Transnational Corporations and Land Speculation in Brazil*. São Paulo: Outras Expressões. <social.org.br/images/MATOPIBA_EN.pdf>.

Prado Jr., Caio. 2007. *A questão agrária no Brasil*. São Paulo: Editora Brasiliense.
____. 1970. *História econômica do Brasil*. São Paulo: Editora Brasiliense.
RádioAgência NP. 2011. "Primeiro resgate de trabalhadores escravizados em colheita mecanizada ocorre no país." December 22.
Ramos, Pedro. 2011. "Financiamentos subsidiados e dívidas de usineiros no Brasil: Uma história secular e … atual?" *História econômica & história de empresas,* 14, 2. <redib.org/Record/oai_articulo3226456-financiamentos-subsidiados-e-d%C3%ADvidas-de-usineiros-brasil-uma-história-secular-e-atual>.
____. 2007. "O uso de mão-de-obra na lavoura canavieira: Da legislação (agrária) do Estado Novo ao trabalho super-explorado na atualidade." In *Anais II Seminário de História do Açúcar: Trabalho População e Cotidiano*. São Paulo: Editora do Museu Paulista da USP.
Rawlins, Omri N. 1980. *Introduction to Agribusiness*. Englewood Cliffs, NJ: Prentice Hall.
Rede Brasileira de Pesquisa em Soberania e Segurança Alimentar. 2021. *National Survey of Food Insecurity in the Context of the Covid-19 Pandemic in Brazil*. <olheparaafome.com.br/VIGISAN_AF_National_Survey_of_Food_Insecurity. pdf>.
Rede Social de Justiça e Direitos Humanos. 2021a. "Ribeirinha community conquers collective right to land." <social.org.br/en/articles/articles-english/281-ribeirinha-community-conquers-collective-right-to-land>.
____. 2021b. "Social mobilization guarantees permanence of Gamela Indigenous people in their territory in Piauí." <social.org.br/en/articles/articles-english/256-social-mobilization-guarantees-permanence-of-gamela-indigenous-people-in-their-territory-in-piaui>.
____. 2020. "PODCAST: Aqui é o meu lugar - resistência das comunidades rurais aos impactos do agronegócio." July 27. <social.org.br/livros-2/37-podcasts/246-podcast-aqui-e-o-meu-lugar-resistencia-das-comunidades-rurais-aos-impactos-do-agronegocio>.
Repórter Brasil. 2011. *O etanol brasileiro no mundo: os impactos sócio-ambientais causados por usinas exportadoras*, May. <reporterbrasil.org.br/documentos/ Canafinal_2011.pdf>.
Ribeiro, Helena. 2008. "Queimadas de cana-de-açúcar no Brasil: efeitos à saúde respiratória." *Revista de Saúde Pública,* 42, 2 (April).
Ricardo, David. 1966. *Princípios de economia política e tributação* [On the principles of political economy and taxation]. São Paulo: Editora Nova Cultural.
Rockefeller Foundation Archives. 1976. *International Basic Economy Corporation Collection*. Projects and Proposals Series, Folder 98, Box 7. Alysson Paulinelli (Minister of Agriculture, 1974–1979). "Carta No. 63 a Rodman C. Rockefeller, March 8, 1976." Sleepy Hollow: Rockefeller Archive Centre.
Ross, Robert L. 2000. *Mission Possible: The Story of the Latin American Agribusiness Development Corporation (LAAD)*. New Brunswick, NJ: Transaction Publishers.
Rosson, Parr C. 1994. *International Marketing for Agribusiness: Concepts and Applications*. Washington, DC: Global Entrepreneurship Management Support.
Roy, Ewell Paul. 1967. *Exploring Agribusiness*. Danville, IL: Interstate Printers & Publishers.

Shiva, Vandana. 1991. *The Violence of the Green Revolution.* Goa: The Other India Press.

Silva, M.A.S. da, N.P. Griebeler, and L.C. Borges. 2007. "Uso de vinhaça e impactos nas propriedades do solo e lençol freático." *Revista Brasileira de Engenharia Agrícola e Ambiental,* 1, 11.

Silva, Maria Aparecida de Moraes. 2002. *Errantes do fim do século.* São Paulo, Editora UNESP.

Smith, Adam. 1988. *A riqueza das nações* [The wealth of nations], Vol. 1. São Paulo: Editora Nova Cultural.

Stefano, Daniela, Débora Lima, and Maria Luisa Mendonça. 2020. *Especulação com terras na região matopiba e impactos socioambientais.* São Paulo: Rede Social de Justiça e Direitos Humanos. <social.org.br/files/pdf/RelatorioREDE_NOV2020.pdf>.

UNCTAD. 2013. *Wake Up Before It Is Too Late: Make Agriculture Truly Sustainable Now for Food Security in a Changing Climate.* Geneva: United Nations. <unctad.org/system/files/official-document/ditcted2012d3_en.pdf>.

United Nations. 2008. *U.N. Declaration on the Rights of Indigenous Peoples.* Geneva: United Nations. <un.org/esa/socdev/unpfii/documents/DRIPS_en.pdf>.

____. 2007. *Basic Principles and Guidelines on Development-Based Evictions and Displacement: Annex 1 of the Report of the Special Rapporteur on Adequate Housing as a Component of the Right to an Adequate Standard of Living:* A/HRC/4/18. February 5. <ohchr.org/Documents/Issues/Housing/Guidelines_en.pdf>.

United Nations General Assembly. 2018. "Resolution 73/165." *United Nations Declaration on the Rights of Peasants and Other People Working in Rural Areas.* December 17. <geneva-academy.ch/joomlatools-files/docman-files/UN%20Declaration%20on%20the%20rights%20of%20peasants.pdf>.

Vergopoulos, Kostas. 1977. "Capitalismo disforme: o caso da agricultura no capitalism." In *A questão agrária e o capitalismo,* eds. Samir Amin and Kostas Vergopolous. Rio de Janeiro: Paz e Terra.

Vogeler, Ingolf. 1981. *The Myth of the Family Farm: Agribusiness Dominance of U.S. Agriculture.* Boulder, CO: Westview Press.

Walker, Richard A. 2004. *The Conquest of Bread: 150 Years of Agribusiness in California.* New York: New Press.

Woolverton, Michael (ed.). 1985. "Introduction." *Agribusiness: An International Journal,* 1, 1 (Spring).

Xavier, Carlos Vinicius, Fábio T. Pitta, and Maria Luisa Mendonça. 2011. *A Monopoly in Ethanol Production in Brazil: The Cosan-Shell Merger.* São Paulo: Editora Outras Expressões. <social.org.br/index.php/pub/booklets-english/139-social-and-environmental-impacts-of-sugarcane-production-in-brazil.html>.

Index

storage, 10, 26
in agribusiness system, 21–2, 34–5
subsidiaries, 60
agricultural control, 62–4, 79, 81
establishing global, 5, 24–5, 38, 55,
73
subsidies,
agribusiness dependence on, 18–19,
32–5, 43, 48–50, 80–4, 97
corporate seeking of, 4–7, 58–9, 76,
83
subsistence, 3
food production for, 46–7, 95
loss of means of, 43, 70
sugar industry, 28
Brazilian, 22, 27, 54–7, 62, 73–84,
86–7
debt, 7, 58–61, 73–4, 77, 83–4
ethanol production, 6–7, 61, 75–84,
86–8
labour exploitation, 86–7, 89–98
plantations, see plantations
supermarkets, 16, 35, 37

Teachers Insurance and Annuity
Association (TIAA)
Brazilian agribusiness and, 61–5,
79–81
subsidiary companies, 62–4, 79–80
see also Cosan; Nuveen
technological revolution, promotion of,
1, 9, 38
theory of value, 2–3, 40, 44, 48
total recoverable sugar (TRS), 88
trade, agricultural,
free, see free trade
monopolies, 2–4, 19, 26, 37–8,
71–2
surpluses, 7, 30, 58
transportation, 42, 83, 86, 97–9
in agribusiness system, 9, 13–14, 35,
53, 95
company mergers, 19, 21, 26
of workers, 89, 92

UN Committee on the Elimination of

Discrimination Against Women
(CEDAW), 95–6
UN Economic Commission for Latin
America and the Caribbean
(ECLAC), 23
United States, 59–60, 97
agribusiness policies, 1–2, 9, 19,
33–4
agricultural exports, 12–13, 17,
32–5, 83, 98
corporations, dominance of, 2,
24–5, 28–9, 61–2, 72, 79–82
foreign policy priorities, 17–18,
21–3, 56–7
geopolitical interests, 14–18, 51,
53–4, 72
role in agribusiness expansion, 2, 5,
9–11, 32–9, 99
urban areas, 30
in capitalist system, 47–8, 94
migration to, 27, 38, 55–8, 70
poverty in, 29, 52, 57, 100
US Agency for International
Development (USAID), 20, 25, 38,
39n1
US Department of Agriculture (USDA),
12, 14, 33, 36
use value, exchange value versus, 2–3,
40–2

Vergopoulos, Kostas, 45

water,
agribusiness impacts on, 5–7,
59–60, 66–7, 75
biodiversity and, 65–6, 85–6
commodification of, 2, 41–2, 52, 77
Indigenous/rural struggles for,
67–9, 95–6, 100
intensive use of, 4, 38, 86, 98
policies for conservation, 13
pollution, 24–5, 39, 47–9, 79, 95
privatization of, 41, 47, 52, 73, 85
workers' supply of, 90–3
wheat, 17, 19
industrial production of, 12, 28, 37,